THE
MOTHER OF JESUS

THE
MOTHER OF JESUS

BY

CHANOINE HENRI MORICE
Docteur ès-Lettres

THIRTY-ONE READINGS

FOR THE MONTH OF MARY

AND THE MONTH OF THE HOLY ROSARY

Translated
by
CLARA MEIGS SANDS, R.S.C.J., M.A.

1826

P. J. KENEDY & SONS

PUBLISHERS   NEW YORK

𝔑𝔦𝔥𝔦𝔩 𝔒𝔟𝔰𝔱𝔞𝔱

ARTHUR J. SCANLAN, S.T.D.
Censor Librorum

𝔍𝔪𝔭𝔯𝔦𝔪𝔞𝔱𝔲𝔯

✠ FRANCIS J. SPELLMAN,
Archbishop, New York

April 1, 1940

FOREWORD

One is amazed, on glancing through the Publishers' Catalogues, to see the number of works devoted to the Blessed Virgin. Each pays its tribute of homage to Mary; and these voices rising from all sides in the Catholic world, blend in a symphony whose volume is constantly increasing.

Again to speak of Mary, after so many theologians, orators, poets, . . . is it not sheer audacity? Can anything new be said on a subject thousands of times treated? Yet we can not resist the desire to add our little note to the Marian Concert. However weak it be, it may have a special quality, for each one adores and sings according to his own nature.

In these meditations we have emphasized the striking resemblance between Jesus and His Mother. They have the same thoughts, the same feelings, the same character. In the Magnificat, we might think we were listening to an anticipated echo of the Sermon on the Mount. Why should this surprise us, since Mary was at once the teacher and the disciple of Jesus? Humanly speaking, they interpenetrate each other.

To instruct us concerning these divine relations, we have but one document, laconic enough, to our way of thinking!

Foreword

What the Gospel records of the Virgin Mary fills few pages. But in this concision, what riches! What a presentiment of marvels it evokes! It might be said of the mysteries of Mary as of the mysteries of Jesus, that they are "cantos of the poem of eternal Love." [1] Of this poem composed by God, we know but a few passages, passages, however, of such beauty as to make us envy the elect who contemplate it with admiration in its entirety. Thus when a beggar passes a house brightly lighted for a ball or party, if a beam of light filters through the shutters to him, he sees in imagination the brilliantly decked hall, and dreams, not without envy, of the pleasure of the guests.

H. M.
Carmelite Tertiary
Chaplain of Notre Dame
at La Roche-Bernard.

[1] Msgr. Gay, Elévations.

TRANSLATOR'S NOTE

Readers of this delightful book, remembering that the distinguished author is a Frenchman, will understand that "our country" is France, and that the pronoun in the First Person Plural always signifies Frenchmen!

That France is "unique" in claiming as Queen the "Glorious and Immaculate Mother of God" will be a surprise to many who know that Hungary has claimed that honor for centuries; that Bavaria also hailed Mary as Queen, even before that country had become a Kingdom! Both these countries added to the end of the Litany of Loretto, after the invocations in the "Regina" section, "Regina Ungariae" and "Regina Bavariae" respectively. The National Flag of Bavaria was light-blue and white, Mary's colors, the Knights of St. George, the Highest Order to which Bavarian nobles could aspire, wore in full dress a most exquisite costume of blue and white. In the style of Louis XIV, with white silk stockings and white satin kneebreeches, white satin waistcoat heavily embroidered with silver, and a knee-length coat of a light-blue velvet likewise embroidered and frogged with silver, they wore on the greatest occasions a long mantle of light-blue velvet, silver-trimmed, the train of which was carried by pages in blue and white.

Translator's Note

In the Corpus Christi Procession, they marched immediately after the Royal Family and Princes of the Blood,
following the Blessed Sacrament.

The Bavarian Steamers plying on the Lake of Constance
were always painted blue and white, the boundary-posts
were blue and white, no one could forget that Bavaria
was Mary's country. What is done *now*? Perhaps things
have not wholly changed.

Clara Meigs Sands, r.S.C.J.

TABLE OF CONTENTS

Table of Contents

NOS CUM PROLE PIA BENEDICAT VIRGO MARIA!

THE
MOTHER OF JESUS

I

The Annunciation

THE simplicity of the Gospel conceals astonishing riches. One never wearies of meditating upon it. It is a mine, where the deeper one digs, the greater the treasure one discovers.

Let us reread attentively, pondering the sense of every word, the account of the Annunciation. We shall find in it the first sketch, as it were, of Mary's character. She appears here, as we shall find her later, with her eminent virtues, her virginal purity, her prudence, her utter abandonment to the Divine Will.

Betrothed, but not yet married, the Virgin was living with her parents. The scene takes place then in the house of Anna and Joachim, visited by every pilgrim to the Holy Land. What a thrill runs through them as they read on the pavement the inscription which reminds them of the sublimest mystery of our Faith and the greatest of all historical events:

The Mother of Jesus

Hic, de Maria Virgine, Verbum caro factum est.

Here, of the Virgin Mary, the Word was made Flesh.

A fresco by Fra Angelico in the Convent of San Marco in Florence, represents Gabriel delivering his message. He is standing, his head slightly bent, his arms crossed on his breast, in an attitude of deepest respect. By his nature he is far superior to this young girl; is not the human soul the lowest rung in the ladder of spirits? But her rank as Mother of God will lift Mary to the highest place among all creatures and in her the Archangel reveres his future sovereign.

He feels attracted towards this soul, so pure, so detached from things of the senses. What amazes heavenly spirits is our fondness for material things. How can we prefer worthless goods to Perfect Beauty? And yet, the fact remains; what is tangible and visible fascinates us. We are more impressed by the brightness of a lamp than by the shining of the stars.

We love least what we should love most, which results in so many aberrations, so many falls! But in Mary there is none of this strange confusion. God reigns in her: He is always the best loved, the first served. And the Angel admires this straightforward, wholehearted, spiritual nature, akin, nay, the sister of his own. He does not at once announce the momentous news to her. He does not flash before her eyes a light that would dazzle her. With the delicacy befitting an Ambassador of Heaven, he leads her little by little to a glimpse of the truth. "Hail!" he says, "full of grace!"

To prepare the Virgin for her mission, God has filled her with graces. She is the most perfect of women and will be the most glorious. Such is the condition of her dignity and its reward. But in what does this dignity itself consist? The Archangel explains it in these words: "The Lord is with thee," words which may be interpreted in two ways: God loves you, or God dwells in you.

At these words, the chaste Virgin is troubled and wonders what this salutation means. Yet its meaning is quite clear. But the apparition of this personage, so beautiful, so imposing, so mysterious, intimidates her. What are his secret intentions? What is he leading up to?

The Angel guesses her emotion; "O Mary," he says, "fear not!" He pronounces for the first time that sweet name which in the course of centuries will hover on the lips of men and be glorified by the choirs of Angels; blessed name which sums up all that we can conceive as most pure, most noble, most ideal.

In a few words chosen from all eternity by Him Whose trusted messenger he is, Gabriel announces to Mary that she will become a mother; he reveals to her the name, the mission, the glory of her Son. He will be great, He will reign for ever over the House of Jacob.

What a perspective for the humble Virgin! It is said that: "every man wants to beget his own double." It is only half true. Life, like flame, always tends upward. Parents want their children to be richer, more honored, happier than themselves, that they may carry on the upward trend of the family. Now the Son of Mary will be King; He will sit upon the throne of David, His forefather. He will use His power only for the relief of human misery; He will be called the Saviour of the world. Crowds will acclaim Him, and something of His glory will be reflected upon His Mother. Marveling at His eloquence, the woman of Galilee will cry out: "Blessed is the womb that bore thee, and the breast that gave thee suck!"

Nevertheless, at the sight of this magnificent future opening out before her, Mary does not seem elated. Mistress of herself, wise, prudent, she reflects. At last she questions the heavenly messenger: "How shall this be done? . . ."

Gabriel then explains to her that the child to be born of her will have no earthly father. She will form and bring Him into the world without detriment to her virginity. Thus Mary's greatness surpasses all that she could imagine.

To be Mother of the King of Israel, Mother of the Messias, is too little for her: she is to be Mother of God.

And how doubt the Angel's word, since he gives her a sign that she can verify: "And behold, Elizabeth, thy cousin, at her advanced age, considered barren by everyone, is now in her sixth month." God's power knows no limits. Mary has but one word to say, a "yes" and great things will be done in her.

What a prodigious elevation! Hitherto the daughter of Anna and Joachim has led a humble life, dividing her days between prayer and household duties. And behold she is offered an honor which the most ambitious woman would not dare covet.

But what will it cost, this transcendent honor? At the sight of this peak to which she is suddenly raised, Mary is seized with terror, a sort of vertigo comes over her. She thinks of her affianced, of the trials awaiting her. Every dignity is a burden, everything has to be paid for. The Virgin knows it. But is it not a duty to accept the mission that God confides to her? His slightest wish is a command for her. So she no longer hesitates, and with absolute abandonment of her whole being, she casts herself into the abyss of glory and of suffering: "Behold the Handmaid of the Lord, be it done unto me according to thy word."

This *Fiat* of Nazareth recalls that of Gethsemane. Overwhelmed with disgust and dread, the Son of God, in agony, beseeches His Father to spare Him the bitter chalice; but understanding that He must drink it for the salvation of the world, He bows His Head and murmurs: "Not My will but Thine be done!"

Here we discern clearly a trait of resemblance between Jesus and His Mother. In virtue of what is called heredity, parents transmit to their descendants a family likeness, peculiarities of temperament or character. When He was forming Mary's mind and heart, God conformed to the law which He Himself had established. He bestowed upon her the virtues which were to shine with such splendor in Christ. Mary was the Dawn of the Sun of Justice, she was the beginning of Christ. Are not the words of Jesus; "My meat is to do My Father's Will." the echo of her reply to Gabriel?

Mary's *Fiat,* like that of Jesus, bears the mark of resignation rather than of enthusiasm. But it is not a gloomy resignation, not the sullen acceptance of the worst that could happen. No, it is a joyful acquiescence inspired by love. It does not cost to serve when one loves. A war-widow, Mireille Dupoucy, said to a friend: "When one has lovingly consented to His Will, it matters little what the Master's good pleasure has in reserve for one. It becomes impossible to suffer in obeying Him. Everything is changed into acts of love, and consequently into joy."

Like the *Fiat lux* of Creation, Mary's *Fiat* did, by divine power, what it signified. The Word became Incarnate in her virginal womb. She became an Ark of the Covenant, a thousand times holier than that built in the desert by Moses' order. After all, that ark, before which the Jews prostrated themselves trembling with awe, contained only the Tables of the Law and a little Manna, while Mary bore within her the Author of the Law, Him of Whom the Manna was but a feeble figure.

The Feast of the Annunciation might then equally well be called the Feast of the Incarnation, and one is surprised that it does not awaken more echoes in Christian souls. More even than the other mysteries, the Incarnation reveals to us the infinite goodness of God. Between the humiliations of the Crib and those of Calvary and the Eucharist, the distance, be it ever so great, is limited, finite, but what relation is there between the Creator, the Sovereign Master of Heaven and earth, and an imperceptible germ forming in the womb of a virgin? On the day of the Annunciation, God reduced Himself to Nothingness; St. Paul was to write: He annihilated Himself.

This momentous event was accomplished in a few instants, but its consequences are incalculable; through age after age they continue to unfold, they will resound for all eternity. Such is the importance of this mystery, that the Church celebrates it not merely by an annual Feast, but daily, thrice. When the Angelus rings from every belfry in the Catholic world, the faithful make the Sign of the Cross, and their thoughts go back to the humble village where God made Himself man. How did the Infinite assume the form of an infinitesimal germ? We do not understand how, but we believe in Love. God loves according to His Nature, that is to say, immensely, immeasurably, infinitely. Therefore when He willed to manifest Himself to men He gave them a gift, I say not princely or royal, but divine, a gift which is naught else but His Son Himself. *Sic Deus dilexit mundum.*

II

Jesus Living in Mary

MARY has no sooner pronounced her Fiat than the mystery of the Incarnation is wrought in her; a mystery of annihilation and love; the Infinite sets Himself limits, and the Eternal begins; primordial mystery, the necessary condition of several others, for since the Son of God willed to dwell amongst us, to die for our salvation, to give Himself as food, it was necessary that He should assume flesh like unto ours, and it was in Mary's womb that this stupendous union of the divine and the human natures was affected.

What were the relations of Jesus and His Mother during the time that elapsed between the Annunciation and the Nativity? Although the Gospel says little about this, Christian thought returns to it constantly: it is an abyss into which one delights to plunge.

WHAT JESUS GIVES TO MARY.—To the fruit of her womb a mother gives the best of her substance, but she expects and receives nothing from him. It is otherwise with the germ that is imperceptibly developing in the virginal womb! He formed His Mother before being formed by her.

Enamored of His own beauty, beloved by His Father, adored by the Angels, the Son of God enjoyed perfect bliss. Moved with pity for us, He cast Himself down from high heaven into the gulf of our misery. Soon He will be exposed to misunderstanding, to ingratitude, to the hatred of those He comes to save. Prodigious abasement! But before reaching its final stage, as if He wished to accustom Himself to His new life, He lays Himself in His first cradle, His Mother's womb. It is the halt before the battle.

Everyone pictures to himself, with mingled joy and desire, the creature he would fain love, her who fulfills his dearest aspirations. It is, alas! but a mental image, a dream. But Jesus, because He was God, made His ideal a reality. He gave Himself a Mother after His own Heart. He adorned Her with virtues that He might take pleasure in her.

As the Litanies say, she is the Mirror of Justice, the image of the divine perfections, the calm and limpid ocean in which is reflected unbroken the azure of an exquisite sky. She is the House of Gold, so radiant, so brilliant, that she seems pure light; she is a Tower of Ivory, precious in substance, perfect in form; she is an Eden, flowery and fragrant, the terrestrial Paradise of the new Adam. She is a Heaven, where He tastes the joy of being loved with whole-hearted tenderness.

St. John of the Cross, in his Spiritual Canticle, compares Him to a Magician, who by the power of his glance beautifies the spots where he passes:

> O groves, O leafy, verdant bowers,
> Planted by the Beloved's Hand,
> O meadow, lush and green with grass,
> With bright-hued blossoms pied,
> Tell me, has He passed this way,
>   He Whom I love?
>
> Scattering a thousand graces
> Through these groves He passed in haste,
> And by His mere glance,
> By His countenance alone,
> He left them clothed with beauty,[1]

[1] A free rendering of these stanzas from the *Song of the Soul and the Bridegroom* develops the thought:

The Soul.

O ye trees of trackless forests,
And ye thickets of the land,
Shade and shelter for the weary
    Planted by his loving hand,

O ye meadows, fresh and verdant,
Pictures of the land above,
Decked with flowers bright and
    fragrant,
    Tell me, have you seen my love?

The Creatures Answer.

We have seen Him! We have seen
    Him!
O! the beauty of His Face!
Moving through the groves, and
    pouring
Down the treasures of His grace.

Hastening on, He looked upon
    them,—
O! that look! how full of love!—
And the groves became more lovely,
    With a beauty from above.

These stanzas are taken from *The Living Flame of Love,* by St. John of the Cross, with his Letters, Poems, and Minor Writings. Translated by David Lewis. London. Thomas Baker. 1934.

13

If the countryside can be transfigured by a single glance, what shall we say of the sanctuary where the Son of God dwelt for nine months?

WHAT MARY GIVES TO JESUS,—is the instrument which He will use to accomplish His work. She fashioned that adorable Heart, the purest, the tenderest, the most generous that ever beat in a human breast. She gave Him the Blood which was to flow on Calvary; that inexhaustible fountain which, branching out through the channels of the sacraments, will freshen and fertilize the world. She formed the first eyes of flesh through which the Creator looked upon His work; the lips which pronounced sublime words by which we still live; the hands, which after healing so many sick, were nailed to the Cross; in preparing our Victim, she was already beginning the work of our salvation. The poet, Brizeux, writes:

> Fair marble forms, mirrored in the fountain's clear
>   and tranquil pool,
> Reflect their beauty to the downcast eyes of youthful
>   mothers
>   As they shyly pass;
> And these then all unconsciously their precious bur-
>   den mould
>   Upon these types of perfect loveliness.

14

Upon what model did Mary fashion the body of Jesus? No living creature, no masterpiece of art was worthy to serve as model. The beauty of Jesus eclipsed all else. But the divine Artist was working in her, creating the Man above all men excellent, the progenitor of a new humanity. Mary provided the matter for His work, blood which original sin had not polluted by any germ of death. She was God's collaborator. Thus little by little was built up, in hiddenness and silence, a marvel which would have dazzled the world,—had the world comprehended it.

MARY'S FEELINGS TOWARDS THE CHILD SHE BORE.— The Saviour of the world belonged to all. That is why He wished to be born, not in a private house, but in a cave, open to all who came. That is why He died in the open air, on a hill, in full view of the inhabitants of Jerusalem and of all the pilgrims assembled for the Pasch. The gift of God was to become the property of men. But from His conception until His birth, Jesus belonged entirely and exclusively to His Mother. She could say: "My Beloved is Mine and I am His." Rapturous union of God and His creature! Intimacy until then unprecedented!

According to the Epistle to the Hebrews, the first act of the Incarnate Word was the oblation of Himself: "Behold I come to do Thy Will, O God!" In Mary's womb,

His first temple, He performs a priestly function. Before Him, priests had been sinful men, often distracted and negligent. They could not comprehend the depth of their misery, nor the infinity of the divine perfections. But Jesus knows His Father, because He is consubstantial with Him. Being perfection itself, He does all things well, and renders to God a worship worthy of His Majesty.

Mary associates herself with the divine Adorer. She joins her voice to the ineffable canticle He sings in her. She repeats with Jesus what He says to His Father.

She adores Jesus Himself. Has she not the right and the duty to do so, since He is the Son of God? In excess of fondness, mothers sometimes say to their children: "I adore you." In their case it is a mere figure of speech, but for Mary, it was a reality. Alone of all creatures, she could literally adore her Child.

With mystics, the feeling of the presence of God is not simply an act of faith; it is, at least at intervals, an experience, a contact, which stirs them to the very depths of their being. To prolong this delightful ecstasy, were it but for a moment, they would willingly endure a thousand deaths. Was this ecstasy not Mary's habitual state? God living in her made her feel His presence. Before the abyss of His perfections, she was transported with joy, like one of the elect on the threshold of Heaven.

Every mother loves the child she is about to bring forth. But she loves him without knowing him. He is but an ideal whom she invests with qualities more or less imaginary. Mary, on the contrary, did know the Child to Whom she was about to give birth. The Archangel had revealed to her His Name, His Mission, His Future Greatness. Who can even imagine the colloquies she had with Him in the recollection that was the atmosphere of her pious dwelling!

"O my Child, I love Thee with all my soul. My Will shall be Thine. I shall have no joy but Thy good pleasure. Oh! how I should like to have all the riches of the world to offer to Thee!" And Jesus might make answer: "Am I not infinite power? What do I want with material goods which I created with a single word? What I prize far more is what human liberty can give or refuse: Love. O Mother, thou lovest Me with a tenderness, an ardor that will never be equaled. Be thou blessed amongst all women!"

In presence of the Host, that white robe that covers the humanity of Christ, is there anyone that has not felt at sometime a sort of impatience? We would like to remove this veil, and to behold Him Whom we adore without seeing. She also possessed a treasure, but a hidden treasure. When would she see that Face, so like her own but with more of majesty, more of the celestial? When would she be able to follow in His glance, in His smile, the emo-

17

tions of His soul? Thus her days passed in peaceful wait-
ing, sure of being satisfied at last.

Miserable creatures that we are, we share, nevertheless,
in Mary's dignity. During our Communion, Jesus is living in us as He lived in her. The only difference is that
He visits us in His glorified state and completely formed.
Ah! if we could "realize" this marvel! We believe it,
doubtless, but it is so beautiful that we dare not let our
thoughts dwell upon it. We turn our eyes away from a
height that would give us vertigo. We forget that God
loves us according to His nature, i.e., infinitely. When
He wished to manifest His love for men, He gave them a
gift worthy of Himself: His Only Son. God is ours, God
is in us: if our faith were more lively, this thought would
make us delirious with joy.

Sully Prudhomme, when dying, said to one of his col-
leagues, recently converted: "Ah! Coppée, how happy
you are to believe!" Yes, how happy Christians would be,
if they were aware of their dignity!

III

THE MAGNIFICAT

WHEN we have lost a relative, we prize the least relic of him: a portrait, a lock of hair. If he has left letters, a private Diary, we love to read and reread these pages which are to us the reflection of his soul.

Alas! no painter, no sculptor has preserved Mary's features for us. We possess no particle of her body, since she was taken up to heaven on the day of her Assumption. But she herself has expressed her soul in a poem so beautiful that even today it is chanted by millions of voices and will continue to be sung to the end of time.

Mary led a humble, hidden life; she is the living source at the bottom of Jacob's Well. Brief and rare are the words recorded in the Gospel as spoken by her. But one day, in Elizabeth's house, the emotions which were overflowing her heart were poured out in a song, a lyric chant. As a daughter of David and heiress of his art and his piety, she improvised a psalm; or rather, she was on that day the organ of the Holy Ghost, a living harp from which He drew divine chords.

The Mother of Jesus

What strikes us at once in this canticle, is the similarity between the soul of Mary and the soul of Jesus. The Magnificat is a prelude to the Gospel. In several of its verses we recognize a forecast echo of the Sermon on the Mount. It leads us to surmise the doctrine and the soul of Jesus.

I. Happy are the rich, happy the strong, happy the victorious! were the maxims current among the pagans. For them happiness consisted in the possession of material goods. But what is the real value of health, wealth, power, —of all that Pascal calls "the grandeur of the flesh"? What are all things that are not eternal?

God alone is great, for nothing is great in the absolute sense of the word, but the infinite. Our whole capacity, therefore, comes from God. A drop of water may swell ever so much, it still remains a drop of water. But let a sunbeam penetrate it, illumine it, it seems a pearl.

Our moral worth is measured by our intimate union with God. The more united with God a soul is, the more she loves Him, the more perfect she is and the happier. But charity grows in inverse ratio to self-love and attachment to perishable things. God hastens to fill the void dug by renunciation. "Where is God?"—"Where self is not."

The author of the Imitation is then right when he says: "Leave all, and thou wilt find all." Renounce the finite and the infinite will be your portion. Those who practice renunciation are the truly wise; they are on the road of perfection and of beatitude. Therefore Jesus glorified them. Blessed are the poor in spirit, blessed are those who mourn, blessed are those who hunger and thirst after justice!

This doctrine, which has produced a veritable revolution in the moral order, is already sketched in the Magnificat. Mary had formulated beforehand the Gospel paradoxes whose application she beheld in her life. Why has the Almighty and Merciful Lord cast His eyes upon her? Because she has humbled herself before Him and proclaimed herself His Handmaid. *Respexit humilitatem ancillae suae.* He that humbleth himself shall be exalted. Later Jesus will call a fisherman of Tiberias, a poor boatman, and will make him the head of His Church. In the Kingdom of God the last shall be first. "He hath filled the hungry with good things and the rich He hath sent empty away." *Et exaltavit humiles.*

II. When God causes them to feel His Presence, mystics experience transports they can not contain. St. Peter of Alcantara, St. Teresa, would have liked to live in a desert so that they might shout for joy. This interior jubilation, this sort of delightful spiritual intoxication which took them out of themselves, gives us some faint idea of the habitual state of the soul of Jesus. He sees always the Face of the Father Who is in Heaven. Even on the Cross, He enjoyed the Beatific Vision. His life was a perpetual ecstasy.

The union of Mary with the Incarnate Word was not so intimate as that of the human and divine natures in the Person of Jesus. Nevertheless, God lived in her and filled her with light and joy.

On fine days we admire the brilliant sunshine sparkling on lakes and seas. Yet what our eyes perceive is but an infinitesimal portion of the ocean of light radiated unceasingly by the sun in every direction. But the light that shone in Mary was not merely a reflection of the Sun of Justice, but that divine Sun Himself. The plenitude of the Divinity dwelt in her. Mary might have said:

> . . . . *Quem totus non capit orbis*
> *In mea se clausit viscera, factus homo.*

"He Whom the whole world can not contain, made man, has closed Himself up in my womb."

The ancients called the exaltation of a soul that believed itself possessed and inspired by God *enthusiasm*. What must have been the enthusiasm of the Virgin who had become through the Incarnation a living tabernacle, another heaven! Her joy was immense, like the treasure she possessed. "Et exultavit spiritus meus in Deo salutari meo."

The Magnificat

"There is more joy in giving than in receiving," said Our Saviour. He Himself putting these words into practice, has lavished upon us the most precious gifts. *Dilexit me,* said the great Apostle, *et tradidit seipsum pro me.* Yes, Christ loved us, and to prove His love to us, He delivered Himself up. By His abnegation, by His Sufferings, He ransomed, sanctified, and saved us. He, the Mystical Vine, was to spread over the entire earth, communicating divine life to innumerable branches. Jesus knew this, and He rejoiced in anticipation over the happiness so many creatures would receive from Him.

Mary herself rejoiced to collaborate in an eternal design. In her was realized the promise made to the patriarch: "In thee shall all the nations of the earth be blessed." A descendant of Abraham shall save the world. There is no man of good will who has not, in one way or another, benefited by the Redemption. But who formed the Redeemer? Who gave Him the blood which He shed on Calvary? It was Mary, co-redemptrix of the human race. In giving birth to Jesus, the new Eve likewise gave birth to those who were to be born of Him.

Her virginal womb is "the hall of the divine sacraments, where Jesus Christ and all His elect were formed." [1]

[1] From the *Treatise on True Devotion to the Blessed Virgin* by Blessed Grignon de Montfort.

The Mother of Jesus

It is, therefore, with good reason that Elizabeth congratulates her: *Beata es, Maria!* and this praise will be repeated from age to age by all generations of Christians. Glory to Mary, through whom all good things come to us! *Beatam me dicent omnes generationes!*

Those who do not share our faith make a great deal of human dignity. But in what does this dignity consist? If, as they claim, life is but an *ignis fatuus,* a tiny flame blown about by the winds, to be eventually extinguished for ever, we do not see what value it has. Some contend that human dignity consists in the power to think. By thought we are superior to the universe; for if the universe contains us, we do more, we comprehend, we *grasp,* it. This is true, in a sense. Nevertheless, we can object with Bossuet: "A building is not more solid than its foundation, nor an accident inherent in a being more real than the being in which it inheres." If our substance is nothing, or little, our faculties and their effects are of still less value.

What then is the foundation of human dignity? It is the indwelling of God in us. Like the Virgin Mary, the Christian in the state of grace is the sanctuary in which abides the Holy Trinity. Like Mary, we are the dwelling-place of a God Who loves us beyond all measure, and Who, in order to love us more, continually perfects us, transforming us to His image, making us share in His

24

nature. We shall, like our God, live eternally and by the same life. What a perspective! The Christian, conscious of his privileges, feels the need of rendering thanks to God, and to express his gratitude, he borrows from the Blessed Virgin the words of her Canticle: *Magnificat anima mea Dominum.*

IV

THE NATIVITY OF CHRIST

IT IS from the Birth of Christ that we reckon time. Unbelievers themselves conform to this custom, and thus, when signing their letters, their receipts, etc., they unintentionally attest that the Birth of the Divine Child is the most important event in history.

Let us try to picture, according to the Gospel and the best authorities on the Scriptures, the circumstances of this greatest of all events. Our attention will centre chiefly upon the Virgin Mary, the beloved Mother of Our Saviour: *Salve, Porta, ex qua mundo lux est orta!* "Hail, O Gate, through which light hath come forth unto the world!"

Bethlehem, where Christ was born, lies to the south of Jerusalem. All around it stretch terraced gardens, planted with fig and olive trees and festooned with vines. It is a smiling oasis amidst dry, naked mountains, like a tuft of flowers and verdure growing by chance in the cleft of a rock. King Solomon loved this country, the native soil of the House of David, his father. He had a magnificent garden laid out there, the site of which is still called, in memory of the Canticle of Canticles, "the Garden Enclosed." Here also he had a vast reservoir constructed to contain the waters of a spring that gushed forth from the depths of a grotto; and these limpid waters, flowing through surface channels as far as Jerusalem, were a figure of the streams of grace, which, pouring from the Cave of Bethlehem, would fertilize and purify the world.

Well now, let us go back twenty centuries in time and take our stand in the city of David in the first year and on the first day of our era. Along a narrow, rocky path leading up to the town, two travellers are pushing forward. One is a man of mature age carrying on his shoulders a cloak rolled up and some provisions. He is leading by the bridle an ass, the traditional beast of burden of the Orient, on which is mounted a woman, clothed in a blue tunic, whose face is concealed by a long white veil. Both appear weary. In obedience to an edict of the Emperor, commanding all the inhabitants to be inscribed in their native towns, they have come from distant Galilee. Alas! in the city of their ancestors, they know no friendly home. They are poor, and the poor man is alone everywhere.

Fortunately, at the top of the hill there is a caravanserai where travellers are lodged gratis. They press on, hurrying to this refuge. But when they reach the entrance, what a disappointment! for Joseph, what dismay! Crowds of pilgrims have arrived ahead of them. In the Court they see asses, camels, filling all the space. There and in the galleries, everywhere, luggage is heaped pell-mell, in the picturesque disorder that delights the Oriental. They look, and retrace their steps. They must seek elsewhere a lodging.

How distressed Joseph is! Oh! it is not for himself that he cares! Industrious, hard-working carpenter that he is, a night in the open air has no terrors for him. He is thinking of his companion, so young and near her time. With what anxious eyes he raps at one closed door after another, only to encounter indifference if not hostility in the refusal he meets.

As for the Virgin Mary, silent beneath her veil, she is absorbed in meditation and prayer. Why should she be alarmed when she is bearing with her Him Who feeds the birds of the air, and clothes with splendor the lilies of the field? She lets herself be led by Joseph, or rather, by Providence, whose instrument he is; and as she rides through the crooked streets, silent now save for the click of the ass's hoofs on the cobbles, she is conversing in her heart with the God Whose temple she is. Who could even imagine, much less attempt to describe the sweetness of these intimate colloquies, of this mysterious interchange of thought and feeling between the Son and His Mother! Mary gives Him her tenderness, her blood, every beat of her heart. Jesus, on His side, gives confidence, hope and serenity to His Mother. Thus, despite the darkening night, despite the solitude growing ever more complete, Mary rides on, her soul quite radiant, carrying Heaven behind her lowered eyelids.

At last Joseph heaves a sigh of relief. Further on, at a turn of the road, he has just caught sight of a cave closed by a barricade. It is a place where the peasants of Bethlehem temporarily park their cattle, but at this hour the flocks and herds are pastured at a distance and the stable is unoccupied. It is a wretched shelter, but it affords protection and secures privacy. The sacred group gladly enters. Like an active resourceful man, Joseph makes the best of the place, cleaning it out and tidying it as well and as quickly as possible, and after a frugal meal, Mary lies down to rest on a pile of straw he has arranged for her as a couch.

Meanwhile, night has fallen, one of those beautiful oriental nights, clear, serene, teeming with stars, mysterious, silent. The air is mild. The gardens in the valley exhale delicate and delightful perfume. The earth is holding its breath in expectation. The heavens smile as if in ecstasy! Never have the stars blazed more brilliantly, and their shining eyes seem riveted upon the dark Cave, whence the salvation of the world is about to come forth. And in this silence and mystery, the beautiful hill of Bethlehem seems to rise higher and higher, under the gentle vibration of the stars, as though it were stretching up to Heaven to bring down the Beloved.

Oh! how express the divine charm of that Christmas night! One would need the lyric accents of a St. Augustine and his triumphant exaltation of spirit to celebrate it fitly and worthily. O peaceful Night, blossoming in stars without number! Solemn Night, when the Word of God came forth from the most pure womb of the Virgin Mary as a ray of light issues from a cloud! Marvelous Night, when for an instant the veil was lifted which hides from us the world invisible; when upon earth, closer to Heaven, the Angels fraternize with the children of men! Night like no other, incomparable Night! beginning of a new and more beautiful era; sacred boundary, whence humanity leaps forward to a new and tiumphant career! Mysterious Night! I love thee for thy brightness, but still more for thy darkness and thy silence, for in thy depths I discern the Almighty Hand restoring His work and forming anew in the Christ the first Adam. Let the earth rejoice, let humanity leap for joy at the approach of the Deliverer, and from the hearts of the poor, the oppressed, the sick, sinners, and all those whom the Divine Child is to ransom, let this cry of hope and gladness burst forth exultant: "Noël! Noël! Joy! O Joy! Behold the Redeemer cometh!"

While these things were happening in Bethlehem, in the distance, on a hillside, shepherds were watching their flocks, seated around a big fire whose smoke rose straight up to the sky in the still air. What were they talking about? Doubtless about the famous census ordered by the Emperor, reminding them so brutally that Judea had lost its independence. Their irritated patriotism demanded an avenger. Ah! when would he come, the Messias predicted by the prophets, the envoy of God, consecrated by the holy unction, who was to re-establish the Kingdom of Israel? He must very soon appear, for the time fixed by Daniel had come: "Come down," they said, "come, heavenly Deliverer! Heavens, drop down dew and let the earth bud forth the Saviour!"

While they were thus conversing about their troubles and their hopes, suddenly a bright light broke upon them and enveloped them. A voice was heard, clear, harmonious, so supernatural and sweet that it sent a delicious thrill through their enraptured souls. It said: "Fear not, for behold, I bring you good tidings of great joy, that shall be to all the people. For this day is born to you a Saviour, who is Christ the Lord, in the city of David. And this shall be a sign unto you. You shall find the Infant wrapped in swaddling clothes and laid in a manger." And suddenly the angelic phalanxes, invisible in the darkness, intoned a canticle, that resounded joyously through the still, clear air: "Glory to God in the highest, and on earth peace to men of good will!"

At once, by a common impulse, the shepherds rose: "Come, let us go over to Bethlehem and see this word that is come to pass." And they hastened to Bethlehem, their hearts overflowing with gladness, their eyes aflame with hope. They reach the town, they find it deep in sleep. No light from any window. In the caravanserai they hear nothing but the rumble of a sleeping crowd.

But as they pass the Cave of the Nativity, the shepherds raise a joyful cry: "Here He is, the Child announced by the Angels!" He is in fact wrapped in swaddling-clothes and lying in a manger. From His entrancingly beautiful face streams a supernatural brightness that lights up the dark Cave. Beside Him Mary and Joseph gaze in adoring silence. The shepherds kneel likewise and adore. They do not question how this Child, apparently so frail, will be able to drive out the usurping Romans and deliver the people from servitude. Heaven has spoken, their faith knows no hesitation. The sordid stable appears a temple to them, the manger an altar. And to this new-born Babe, looking at them as though He had been expecting them, they offer their modest presents.

We may, perhaps, have envied the shepherds who were allowed to see with their eyes the Son of Mary Who was also the Son of the Eternal God. But this feeling seems to us childish if we remember that our churches are other Bethlehems, other "Houses of Bread." The lamp that burns day and night before the altar, like a vigil light beside the bed of one who slumbers, attests an august Presence. The tabernacle is truly a Crib where the Son of God reposes, humiliated, annihilated.

Let us think of this, and a prayer will rise from our hearts: "Jesus, God become a Child for love of me, I adore Thee. Ah! that I could speak like Mary, who, because she was Thy Mother, and because she was all-pure, could offer Thee homage worthy of Thee. She was Thy first adorer. Why have I not the melodious voices of the Angels, for the emotions roused by the mystery of a God-made-man are so deep that human language is impotent to express them. Alas! I have neither the tenderness of Mary, nor the enthusiasm of the Angels! I am but a weak creature, doubly miserable by my insignificance and by my sins. I am unworthy to approach Thee. I acknowledge my wretchedness. Before Thee, O perfect Innocence, Splendor of Light Eternal, I see my soul tarnished and

33

sullied by sins. I deplore my weaknesses; I deplore especially my ingratitude and my coldness towards Thee. Divine Child, henceforth, I shall be more generous; and since of myself I have nothing to draw upon, deign to inspire me with courage to be faithful to Thee."

V

THE FIRST NIGHT ADORATION

IT TOOK place during Christmas night, in the Cave of Bethlehem, by the light of the stars. Later on, Christian churches will be multiplied; in every country of the world steeples surmounted by the cross will point heavenward. But the centre from which this new religion radiated was the stable of Bethlehem. In that sanctuary, to all appearances so destitute, yet which opens out to us the Infinite, the Word-made-Flesh had no visible adorers but Mary and Joseph. Outside all was silent. Save the shepherds, informed by the Angels, no one suspected that the Saviour was born.

Mary had the right and the duty to adore her Child. She remembered the words of the heavenly messenger: "the Holy that shall be born of thee shall be called the Son of God."

Many a time in the Temple of Jerusalem she had adored the Eternal God. When, on the eve of the Pasch, the blood of the victims flowed in torrents, when the sacred trumpets resounded, and the priestly orders defiled in gorgeous vesture through the Temple Courts, she prostrated herself in spirit before her Creator. Her feeling towards Him can be summed up in one sentence: "I am the Handmaid of the Lord." Humble, dependent, she had no other thought but to obey Him to Whom she owed everything.

And lo! this omnipotent King leaves His magnificent palace in heaven; He takes the form of a Child; He is there, before her eyes, wailing on a truss of straw! The thought sends a thrill of joy through Mary's whole being, and from her full heart rises a hymn of gratitude.

"I thank Thee, O Eternal God, for having chosen me to be the mother of this Child, Who is also Thine. The mother of a God! . . . Oh! what a mystery! The Infinite, Whom the universe can not contain, has then shrunk in some incomprehensible way into this new-born Infant Whom I can hold in one arm! The Master of heaven and earth, on Whom all depends, and Who depends on no one, now needs me; He could not live two days without my care! The sovereignly happy God Who enjoyed infinite bliss in heaven suffers now, He wails, He weeps . . . Yes, He weeps; just now, with inexpressible emotion, I saw tears gathering in His eyes. When He shows signs of suffering, I take Him in my arms, I rock Him, I speak to Him soothingly, I sing to Him one of the plain-tive old lullabies that my mother, Anna, crooned over my cradle. And then . . . is it not an illusion? . . . it seems to me that Jesus looks at me with a searching, thoughtful look as though an exiled God were thanking the humble creature who is caring for Him. May Thy Name be again blessed, O God! Thou hast done great things to me, . . . and all generations shall call me blessed."

Thus the Virgin's Canticle rises in trembling, bewildered notes, not knowing whether they should take their flight to the world above, or die away at the tiny feet of the sleeping Child. This Canticle of Thanksgiving, . . . or rather, this stammering, . . . ends in silence. The interior words which the Virgin has just murmured are prolonged in endless reverberations; they lose themselves in depths which thought is powerless to plumb . . . and the prayer of the ideal Adorer is but a long, long look fixed upon the annihilated God.

It is, obviously, very difficult for us to enter into the feelings of Mary. We call her the Incomparable Virgin, the One, the Unique, *Virgo Singularis,* . . . Unique, indeed, for she had exceptional relations with the Incarnate Word, being at once His creature and His Mother.

Ovid tells us that veneration and love do not go well together:

The Mother of Jesus

Non bene conveniunt neque in una sede morantur majestas et amor.

This observation does not apply to Mary. Her adoration shaded off into exquisite tenderness; or, better said, it was a maternal tenderness expanded, widened, reaching out to the infinite in the effort to equal its object. Thence flowed an ineffable sentiment that no other has ever known, that no other ever will know.

And yet, is not our feeling for Jesus in the Sacred Host in some sense analogous? In the tabernacle, He is still smaller than in the Crib, poorer, more dependent. He is at the absolute disposal of His priests, who, when they judge it fitting, take Him in the ciborium, lay Him on the lips of the faithful, carry Him to the sick and lock Him again in His humble seclusion. And Jesus lets it be done; He leaves Himself in their hands as He once left Himself in His Mother's.

And when we receive Him in Holy Communion, can we not say like Mary: "My Beloved is Mine, and I am His"? He is ours, our personal property. As long as the sacred species are not consumed, He is one with us.

Hence arise in us towards the God Who stoops to our lowliness, Who gives Himself to us without reserve, sentiments of gratitude, of tender love, I might almost venture

38

to say, of compassion, which the ancients could not even conceive.

Our natural affections tend to what is visible, near, similar to ourselves. We long to render service to our dear ones, to devote ourselves for them. "I seek a friend," said an ancient, "that I may have some one to die for."

If we are like that, how is it possible for us to love a God Who is pure spirit, Who, being invisible, seems to us far away? Our reason is no more able to comprehend Him than a nut-shell can contain the ocean. And what can we add to His perfections or to His beatitude? He has no need either of our gifts or our homage.

Thus might the Jews have reasoned before the Incarnation. But since the Birth of Christ what a transformation in the relations between God and His creature! Jesus is truly the Emmanuel, the God with us. His contemporaries could see Him with their eyes, touch Him with their hands. I am well aware that, in a sense, God is visible in His works, but Nature, which reveals Him, also conceals Him. It is a screen, not a transparency, for the great majority. They stop at appearances. The temple makes them forget the architect. But in Jesus there is no separation between the divine and the human. Our homage is addressed jointly to the two natures united in one Person. His flashing eyes, the charm of His countenance foreshadows the splendors of the Divinity. *Ut, dum visibiliter Deum cognoscimus, per hunc in invisibilium Amorem rapiamur.*

And since He willed to resemble His brethren in all things, since He has shared our infirmities, He needs our assistance. His Mother wraps Him in swaddling-clothes, she nurses Him, she protects Him. We, ourselves, can console Him, defend Him, work for His cause. And our tender love for Him will increase in proportion to our generosity. The more one gives, the more one loves. The more God costs us, the dearer He becomes to us.

And yet how lukewarm our devotion seems compared with Mary's! Every day we grant an audience to God for a few minutes or for some hours; but the rest of our time, . . . ? Do not our worldly occupations make us forget that He is everywhere present? After shining a few minutes the Sun of Justice is hidden in a cloud.

Mary, on the contrary, had Him always before her eyes. She lived but for her Child, thought of nothing but Him, saw everything in relation to Him. *Quidquid aspiciebat, Christus erat.* What made her love doubly tender was the thought that He was flesh of her flesh. Her first look at Him makes one think of the Creator's appraising look at the universe that He had just drawn out of nothingness: God saw all the things that He had made, and they were very good.

40

Her title of Mother gave Mary special rights. She had familiar relations with Jesus, that we could not permit ourselves. The priest kisses the altar, he kisses the paten, he does not dare kiss the Sacred Host. But the Blessed Virgin could touch her Child's lips with her own. Oh! that mother-kiss, at once so religious and so tender, given to a new-born Babe, Who is a God! . . .

VI

The First Look of Jesus

How deep, how ineffable, that first look of the Child, unable as yet to speak, but Who, as God, knew all things! It rested first upon Mary, expressing with mute eloquence admiration, gratitude and pity.

Look of Admiration.—We sometimes wonder why there are so many hidden treasures, so many flowers that blossom and die in pathless forests, so many diamonds from which no sunbeam ever evokes a sparkle. The reply is simple. God made their beauty for Himself, that the world He looks upon might be good in His sight. The beauty of His work is a reflection of His glory. With what joy then Jesus must have gazed upon His Mother, the all-pure, the all-beautiful!

Descended from a line of Kings, a scion of the most illustrious family of Israel, Mary possessed an innate distinction, a personal charm which she transmitted to her Son, Whom later the Jews will call a "Seducer." But how much more precious was the loveliness of her soul! Moral beauty has the same characteristics as physical beauty. What we admire in a flower is its velvety texture, its delicate coloring, its symmetry, the harmonious arrangement of its petals around an axis or centre; in one word, it is the splendor of order.

Now Mary possessed in the highest degree the virtues which Christ was later to preach by word and example. In her reigned perfect order, for her affections were subject to her will, as her will was subject to God. All her powers converged towards their centre, that is, to their principle, which is also their end.

A poet, Albert Semain, has formulated this strange desire:

Like a diamond be my heart in virgin purity,
Like a diamond too in brilliance and in sterility.

There is something morbid in this affection for solitude and sterility. To the diamond, incapable of change, either to increase in size or to reproduce itself, we should prefer the grace and fecundity of the flower.

Now the Mystical Rose was pure and fecund at the same time. In her, by a singular privilege, virginal integrity and maternal love were allied. She unites all that attracts, all that touches the heart of man.

Therefore, in her praise, the Liturgy borrows from Holy

43

Writ the most poetic expressions: "O Virgin! fair art thou as a palm-tree in Gades, . . . and as a plane-tree by the running waters, . . . thou art exalted like a cedar in Libanus, and as a cypress tree on Mount Sion. Thy perfume is that of cinnamon and choice myrrh; with fragrance thou fillest thy dwelling, like unto the rose-gardens in Jericho." (Ecclesiasticus, 24.).

THE LOOK OF GRATITUDE.—Jesus admires in His Mother a masterpiece of divine wisdom and power, the new Eve, the most perfect of women, and thinking of all that He has received from her, His Heart overflows in gratitude.

He is the flesh of her flesh. She has given Him His members, His organs, the body which is necessary for Him in order to accomplish His mission. She is at that moment lavishing upon Him her tender care and love. She is accustoming Him, so to speak, to His new sort of life.

Between the bliss of Heaven and the dreariness of exile, He had need of a place of rest where He could find something of what He had left behind. There above, He had been adored and served by legions of Angels; He contemplated with transport His Father's majestic beauty. Now He was to live in the ugliness and misery of this world, among weak, ungrateful, corrupt men, of whom some will return His love by hatred. A mournful prospect for the most delicately sensitive, the most loving, the most generous of all Hearts!

Happily His Mother is for Him like another heaven, where He tastes the sweetness of being wholly loved. Within her arms, close to her heart, beating in union with His own, He relaxes, He no longer thinks of the labors, the trials that await Him. Later, when He will be reviled, disgraced, betrayed, crucified, He will remember His Mother's caresses, and in her He will love humanity, that strange plant that bears on the same stem heroism and baseness, tenderness and cruelty, exquisite flowers and poisonous fruits.

We ourselves, in our infancy, were protected and cared for; we had nothing to do but live. Therefore we never think without emotion of her who watched beside our cradle, taking upon herself all the troubles of existence, and letting nothing but its joys reach us. But our gratitude must rise higher. The constant wave of tenderness which flowed from Mary's heart into the Heart of Jesus was fed from the torrent of love which ceaselessly and from all eternity pours from one to the other of the Three Divine Persons. Thus when God formed the mother's heart to the likeness of His own, He placed in it first of all, goodness. ("*Loving-kindness,*" as Juliana of Norwich calls it). "Every good and perfect gift cometh from the Father of light." It is therefore He Whom we must praise in every creature, just as it is the sun that gives its lustre to the pearl that we admire.

THE LOOK OF COMPASSION.—A pious picture, known as Our Lady of Perpetual Help, represents Mary carrying in her arms the Divine Child. He is not a new-born Babe, He looks about three or four years of age. To the right, an Angel is showing the instruments of the Passion: the cross, the crown of thorns, the nails, the lance. Frightened by this vision, Jesus clings to His Mother's hand; and Mary, remembering Simeon's prophecy, seems to gaze into the future with sad and searching eyes. Thus, according to this picture, which is said to date from remote antiquity, the Child Jesus knew the death that He would die. But we can go still further and affirm that He immolated Himself in spirit from the first instant of His conception, when He made this prayer, recorded in the Epistle to the Hebrews: "Sacrifice and oblation thou wouldst not, but a body thou hast fitted to Me; Then said I: Behold, I came to do thy will, O God!" In His foresight of His own sufferings, however, He also saw His Mother's. When two souls love each other devotedly, they have all

46

things in common, joys and griefs are shared. Like two opposite mirrors, they reflect their emotions back and forth. Jesus sympathized with His Mother. He knew what she would have to undergo when the hour of separation came. He saw her in advance upon Golgotha, heartbroken by His wounds, crucified with Him; and He looked pityingly upon every pang that He would cause her. When we come into contact with a person threatened with some great and unsuspected misfortune, our compassion is doubled. This was doubtless Mary's case during the days that followed the Nativity. A mist hid from her eyes the Royal Road, the Way of the Cross, which she would have to tread. But the first glance of Jesus discovered it, and perceiving Calvary at its end, He shuddered at the thought of His Mother's anguish.

Assuredly He foresaw also His future exaltation. But in the order of grace as well as in the order of nature, everything has its price. The size of our cross is the measure of our greatness.

Mary was not exempt from this universal, inexorable law. Her dignity was to cost her dear. Jesus loved her, He wished to make her happy; and He was inevitably dragging her down with Him into an abyss of woe. For a loving heart what more cruel necessity! Many of the tears, therefore, that fell from His infant eyes were tears of pity and tender compassion.

What an inexhaustible subject of meditation are the relations between the best of Sons and the tenderest of Mothers! O Jesus, grant that I may see Mary with Your eyes, and love her with Your Heart! May I be to her a second Jesus!

VII

JESUS AT HIS MOTHER'S BREAST

ONE loves to represent the Divine Infant at His Mother's breast. What a charming picture it is! The Babe seems to slumber; His eyes are closed, He seems to be enjoying the sweetness He tastes. His Mother's head is bent over Him with a smile of happiness in His contentment, happiness in sustaining His life, happiness in beholding His growth from day to day.

The milk she is giving Him is formed from her blood. She is actually nourishing Him with her own substance. In later years she will receive Him in Holy Communion, now He is receiving her.

The elements which compose a mother's milk are derived from her daily food and from the air she breathes. When Mary takes her food it is less for herself than for her Child. At every breath she might say to Him: "It is for Thee, Beloved! I am Thine, I live for Thee alone!"

Thus she continues to collaborate in the redemptive design. She is bringing up the Wonder-worker Who will cure all infirmity, heal all disease; the Comforter, Who

49

will soothe countless troubles; the Prophet, Whose words will dazzle the world; the Saviour, Who will ransom it by His death. In performing her maternal function she is preparing our salvation.

She is still nourishing and bringing up the Mystical Body of Christ today. As the universal Mediatrix, the Treasurer of Paradise, all grace comes to us through her. If she is not the source of supernatural life, she is the aqueduct which transmits it to us. It is through her that we are converted, sanctified, saved.

Like her, we must form Jesus Christ in ourselves. The knowledge we have of Him is not sufficiently actual, sufficiently complete, nor sufficiently living. We must constantly add new touches to this interior portrait, freshen it up in some way, revive it unceasingly. This is how Jesus grows in us. Ah! may He fill us entirely, occupy the whole interior room, even if He puts us out of it! "O Jesus!" exclaimed a holy religious, "do You think I can live like this, giving You only bits of myself? . . . When shall I stop being reasonable? . . . When shall I be foolish enough to love You? . . . When shall I love You too much?" [1]

We must also develop the mystical body, and first by

[1] Rev. P. Henrion, S.J., *Journal Spirituel.*

developing ourselves. The value of a whole depends on the value of each of its parts. A stone that has been cut and polished adds to the beauty of an edifice, a bud that blossoms adds to the growth of the vine. Thus every effort towards good enriches the Church. Every act of virtue raises, even though it be only an infinitesimal amount, the level of humanity.

In proportion as we approach perfection, our power of intercession increases, our words are more persuasive, our example more attractive, all our means of action become more efficacious. The great secret of the apostolate is then to love God with all our heart. St. Teresa of the Child Jesus never left her cloister; her external activity was almost nil; yet her beneficent influence was world-wide. Why? Because she had the generous ambition of loving Christ as no one else had ever loved Him. The fruitfulness of her apostolate is accounted for by the intensity of her love.

This is the significance of the star that appears on her coat-of-arms. Stars send out light unceasingly, in all directions, because they are vast conflagrations. The intensity of their fire is the measure of their radiation!

This thought, so often recurring in the writings of the little Saint, is a familiar one to chosen souls. Elizabeth Leseur used to say: "Every soul that rises, lifts the world."

Lucie Félix Faure-Goyau wrote in her private Diary: "It suffices that a heart should break with love, to fill the world with it."

The apostolate by word and by work completes this apostolate of example and personal influence. It is especially exercised in child-training. The parents in the home, the Christian teacher in the school, the priest in the confessional, at the Catechism Class, in the Sodality, try to mould souls to the likeness of Christ.

It is a difficult task, that! The Professor, whose aim is merely to instruct, has the support of very strong natural tendencies: curiosity, emulation, desire to succeed. But the educator properly so called, the one who "brings or leads out," who builds up, finds all the passions in conspiracy against him. How many adolescents are like clay, so soft as to be almost liquid! When one has kneaded it, not without trouble, into a passable shape, it doubles over on itself, and the work has to be done all over again.

However, one must not lose courage. The effort must be proportioned to the importance of the work, to the value of the final results. When Jesus was lying in His Mother's arms, who could have foreseen His marvelous destiny! So, some child, indistinguishable from his comrades by any outstanding quality, may become a genius whose discoveries will transform the economic life of his country; he may become a general who will lead his troops to victory; he may become an intrepid missionary who will convert thousands of pagans. Like the mother of Moses, we may be bringing up saviours. That is well worth some effort, some personal sacrifice.

Sacrifice is the correct word, for there is no apostle without self-forgetfulness, renunciation. "Unless the grain of wheat, falling into the ground, die, itself remaineth alone; but if it die, it bringeth forth much fruit." These words of Christ He confirmed by His example. For three whole years, He traversed Palestine in all directions, preaching to the multitudes, training His apostles, multiplying miracles. For three hours only He hung nailed to the cross; and those three hours of immobility, of apparent inaction, did more for our salvation than three years of the most intense, strenuous activity. It is not action that saves the world, but *passion* in the etymological sense of the word, that is suffering, sacrifice. The saviours are the crucified.

To attain his end, the apostle turns to profit even the least occasion. For him nothing is trivial; a service rendered, an opportune visit, a greeting, a handshake, anything is useful, he makes anything serve his zeal. It is not given to all to perform brilliant acts, but there is no one who is unable to desire ardently the glory of God, to think of it constantly and to refer everything to this end. By self-multiplication, microscopic cells build up powerful organisms; thus the accumulation of the infinitely tiny acts of the apostolate build up the City of God. The share of each worker seems insignificant, even negligible; but the concerted efforts of myriads of hidden apostles produce magnificent results.

O Holy Educatress of Jesus, grant that I may increase, however little, His Mystical Body, even should it require all my time, all my strength, all my resources! *Omnis impendam, et superimpendar ipse pro animabus!* May I labor for God to my last breath!

VIII

MARY'S PIETY

BEFORE the Incarnation Mary's piety consisted in submission, gratitude, humility. To humble herself before the Eternal God, to acknowledge that she owed Him everything, to do His Will gladly, was her habitual disposition. Constantly united to God, she led a pure, holy life.

But after the Incarnation, and especially after the Nativity, her piety assumed another aspect. It was not to the Almighty Father alone that she offered her homage, but to the Infant also, Whom she carried in her arms. She could say to Him, without hyperbole or blasphemy, "I adore Thee." Her prayer consisted in converse with Him, her worship, in caring for Him.

Mary then was the first Christian. In contradistinction to the Jews and the Mohammedans who claim that they deal directly with God, we believe that no one goes to the Father save by the Son. Doubly wretched because of our insignificance and our sinfulness, we feel the need of a mediator. It is through Jesus Christ that we perform acts of religion. The first devotion of the Christian is to the

55

The Mother of Jesus

Incarnate Word, and Mary offers us an admirable model of it.

PIETY INSPIRED BY FAITH.——How did the Virgin know the Divine Nature of Jesus? By Revelation. She had believed the heavenly messenger, or rather, God, speaking by his lips. "Blessed art thou that hast believed!" St. Elizabeth said to her later. It is because she believed the Lord that the world was saved.

Our piety, like Mary's, is penetrated by Faith. For us, Jesus is not merely a historical personage who lived in Galilee in the time of Tiberius, founded a new religion and died under Pontius Pilate. He is the Son of God, conceived of the Holy Ghost, born of the Virgin Mary. Belief in this mystery nourishes and uplifts our piety, as it stretches out to reach its divine object. Alas! it can not lift itself to His level, and never will. Everything is weak in us, even our regret that we love so little. Ah! if only we had a heart like Mary's to love Jesus!

ARDENT LOVE.——What appeals to us above all is something that we can apprehend by the senses, something *sensible,* and Christ in His glorified state is invisible for us. It is true that the Eucharistic Species attest His Presence, but they hide it also; this veil conceals both His humanity and His divinity at once.

56

As for creatures, they ought to speak to us of God, to lift us up to Him. It happens, unfortunately, that we easily allow ourselves to be captivated by their charm. Our eyes are pleased and linger upon them, so that they mask what they should disclose to us. They act as a screen between us and the spiritual world.

For Mary, none of these obstacles existed. She contemplated at leisure the Word made Flesh. Far from distracting her from the divine, the sensible plunged her more deeply, so to say, into its reticences. In the infantile beauty of Jesus, she admired the transcendent beauty of God. She bent over Him as over an abyss of purity, splendor and mystery.

What also animated her piety was her maternal love. Jesus was flesh of her flesh, the protraction of her own personality, something of her very self. She could say: "He is mine." Her adoration was tinged with tenderness. These two sentiments were in mutual harmony, reinforcing each other, like two keyboards coupled, from which a virtuoso draws magnificent chords. No one ever loved Jesus as did the "Unique Virgin." No one can comprehend what she felt at the sight of her Child, Who was also her God.

CONSTANT LOVE.—We have, or at least we try to have, a habitual sense of the Presence of God. But *habitual* does

57

not imply *always conscious*. God is there, ever ready to reappear, but at times He hides Himself below the horizon. We lose contact with Him. A swarm of things claim our attention. Our intention is upright, we want to attain our last end, but the thought of God is not constantly in our mind. Our piety is intermittent.

Mary's piety was one continuous wave, inexhaustible, steady, gushing from her heart. Jesus was with her uninterruptedly, beneath her eyes or in her arms. During the first two or three years of His life, the Infant belonged to His Mother, since He could not do without her care and protection. The fruit was not yet completely severed from the tree, it still needed its sap and its shade.

PRACTICAL LOVE.—"If you knew the gift of God!" said Christ one day to the Samaritan woman. This gift is nothing less than Himself. Having loved us unto the end, He gave Himself, and still gives Himself, wholly, to all and to each, continually and for ever.

Mary corresponded to the divine generosity, not, certainly, by the excellence of her gift, but by the plenitude of her donation. She gave herself without reserve. She looked upon herself as belonging to her Son, as His property, and out of the treasure that He possessed, she offered

Him every day, at every moment, whatever He might desire: her milk, her services, her caresses.

The stable of Bethlehem was dark, . . . damp, perhaps, . . . and cold; but when Jesus nestled, warm and safe, in His Mother's arms, He had all He needed. She took upon herself all the care and anxiety of life, letting nothing but its smooth side touch Him.

Mary knew how to comfort and defend her Child also; with St. Joseph's assistance, she succeeded in eluding the fury of Herod. She was His visible Providence, and He might have said to her: "You are My shelter, My refuge, My shield. Under your protection, the phantoms of the night do not affright Me. I sleep peacefully upon your bosom like a little bird beneath its mother's wing. You guard Me in all My ways; you carry Me in your arms, lest My feet be bruised by the stones in the road. When I suffer, you are at My side, and at My first call, you come to My help. O great-hearted woman, living image of the goodness of God, may you be for ever blessed!"

Many a time, doubtless, we have envied the contemporaries of Jesus, those hands privileged to touch Him, those favored eyes that saw Him! But is not our happiness quite as great? Is not Jesus in our midst, living in the Sacred Host? We can visit Him every day, we can adorn His tabernacles, His altars, His churches. Everything He touches should be dear to us, for according to St. Francis de Sales, "perfect honor extends to the least appurtenances of the one beloved."

Let us also be the consolers of Jesus. Were He not impassible, how He would suffer to be so little loved! How He would suffer to see preferred to Him, paltry creatures, unworthy to be compared to Him! Especially how intensely He would suffer from the strange, monstrous, in a word . . . devilish hatred against Him of the enemies of the Cross! Who will console Him, if not we? May our ardent piety make amends to Him for the offences He receives day and night, at all hours, in all cities, in every town, in every house of the whole world! Let us love Him the more tenderly for those who do not love Him. Let us serve Him more faithfully for those who forsake Him.

He asks us also to defend Him. In many a church, the priests are obliged to remove Him from His tabernacle every evening and to lock Him in a safe. Are not the witnesses of this ceremony reminded of the Virgin Mary carrying her Son into Egypt?

Lastly, let us not forget that, according to the strong expression of Jeanne d'Arc, Christ and the Church are one and the same. In fact, what is the Church but the Mystical Body of Christ, the organ by whose means He continues to sanctify and save the world? To defend the

Church is to defend Him. To work for His cause is to work for Him.

Today Mary is contemplating Jesus in His glory. She is always in the rapture of a mother who after a long separation sees again and presses once more in her arms a beloved child she had believed to be dead; what unutterable emotion, undiminished in freshness and liveliness by lapse of time!

Here below, we have the "face-to-face" in darkness. We adore, beneath the veil of the Host, Him upon Whom Mary rapturously gazes in Heaven. Our eyes and hers are fixed upon the same object. The same love—love for Him —throbs in our hearts. Hence it follows that no matter how far above us she is raised in sanctity and dignity, she seems to be very near to us.

O Mother in heaven, look down graciously upon those who love your Divine Son, and obtain for them the grace to love Him daily more and more!

IX

THE SHADOW OF THE CROSS

IN THE Vatican Museum there is a miniature painted in the Thirteenth Century by an Abbot of Cluny. Like Raphael's fresco called The Dispute on the Blessed Sacrament, it is composed of two superimposed levels. On the lower, the Infant Jesus is seen lying on an altar, between the Virgin Mary and St. Joseph; on the upper, Christ is on the Cross, between His Mother and St. John. The Cross rises exactly above the Crib; and, to emphasize the symbolism still more, the Virgin-Mother is looking up toward the Crucified. Does this not imply that the Crib is an altar, and the new-born Child a Victim? [1]

Painting is the art of speaking to the eyes, and it sometimes does so very eloquently. What depth of doctrine in this simple miniature! It reminds us that the immolation of Christ did not begin in Gethsemane, as one might be inclined to imagine. The Incarnation, the Hidden Life and

[1] See the reproduction of this beautiful miniature in "The Christ of the Golden Legend" (*Le Christ de la Légende Dorée*) by l'Abbé Broussolle, p. 10.

the Public Life, the Passion, the Ascension, the Eucharist are but one and the same sacrifice, prepared, continued, accomplished, accepted, communicated.

And if one goes to the bottom of this truth, we are even constrained to recognize that the great immolation of Christ was not His ignominious and cruel death, but His conception in the Virgin's womb. From the Crib to Calvary is a shorter distance than from Heaven to the Crib. Between the Crib and the Cross there is, on the whole, but a progressive increase of humiliation and suffering; but between Heaven and the Crib, between the Most-High, adored by angels, and the new-born Babe wailing in His Mother's arms, there is the infinite.

The analogies between these two stupendous mysteries are clearly indicated by the painter of the miniature.

When Jesus came into the world, His Mother had nothing to wrap about Him but the few swaddling bands she had been able to carry on the ass, a simple and poor provision. Upon His gibbet, the Divine Crucified is stripped of all covering save the scanty loin-cloth.

The Divine Child is swaddled, His little members closely bound by linen bands; on the Cross, Jesus is fastened by His Hands and Feet and unable to make any movement.

At His birth, Jesus had no one to help Him but Mary

63

and Joseph. Later the shepherds came, then the Magi, and that muster of peoples depicted by Isaias in a magnificent page. But when He appeared in the stable of Bethlehem, He was almost alone. From the height of His gibbet, Jesus descried in the vast throng of His revilers but one small group of faithful friends. Five or six persons at most, . . . that was the Court of this crucified King.

Jesus was not born in a private house, but in a Cave open to any chance passer-by. He died in the open air, outside the city, on a hill, in full sight of the inhabitants of Jerusalem and of the pilgrims assembled for the Pasch, and this He did to show to men that He belonged to all.

These correspondences are too numerous, too precise, to be fortuitous. Nothing happens, not even the fall of a leaf, that is not either willed or permitted: a fortiori, Providence has regulated even to the least detail the great events of our religious History. Every incident is combined with infinite art.

Beside the Crib, therefore, Mary could have a presentiment of Calvary: how could she fail to be impressed by the fact that the Saviour of men was born in obscurity, indigence, destitution? The presentiment, however, became certainty on the day of the Purification.

There was in Jerusalem at that time an old man named

Simeon, who had the gift of prophecy. He came to the Temple, impelled by the Holy Ghost; and perceiving the Child that Mary was carrying in her arms, he felt a strange thrill run through his whole being. "It is He," said he to himself, "it is the Messias whom humanity has been awaiting for so many centuries."

In a transport of enthusiasm, he took the Child, raised it to heaven, and exclaimed: "Now thou dost dismiss thy servant, O Lord, according to thy word in peace; because my eyes have seen thy salvation which thou hast prepared before the face of all peoples; a light to the revelation of the Gentiles and the glory of thy people Israel!" But to this splendid vision succeeds at once an afflicting prediction. The old man's face grows sad, and in a solemn voice he says to the youthful Mother: "Behold this Child is set for the fall and for the resurrection of many in Israel, and for a sign that shall be contradicted. And thy own soul a sword shall pierce."

What a contrast between this scene and the Annunciation where all is so pure and luminous!

> Sorrow is a fruit; God does not make it grow
> Upon a branch too weak as yet to bear it.

The Archangel confines himself to telling Mary that her Son is to be called Jesus, which means Saviour. But

65

this name which expressed His mission, allowed His destiny also to be foreseen. Nothing great can be achieved without great pain. The saviours are the sacrificed.

During the years she spent in the Temple, Mary had seen lambs, doves and pigeons immolated daily, and a principle of the supernatural order was deeply graven in her mind: "Without the shedding of blood there is no remission." She knew besides the words put on the lips of the Messias by the Prophet: "They have given me vinegar to drink. They have dug my hands and my feet, they have numbered all my bones. . . . From the sole of the foot to the top of the head there is no soundness in him. . . . I am a worm and no man." Austere words, which for her took on a terrible significance when she applied them to her Son. The Messias then would not be a powerful, glorious King, such as the carnal-minded Jews imagined, but a man of sorrows. To redeem the world He would have to shed His blood, that most pure blood which His Mother had given Him.

"Wherever Jesus enters, He enters with His Cross, He brings all His thorns with Him and shares them with all those He loves." [1]

Suffering Himself, He was to cause suffering to all those united to Him by ties of blood or friendship. St.

[1] Bossuet.

66

Joseph did not escape this law; he learned by experience what it cost to be the Foster-Father of a God. But, as is natural, Mary sympathized more tenderly, more deeply in the sorrows of her Son. That is why Simeon addressed his prophetic warning to her and not to her spouse, who was not even to be a witness of the Passion.

Apprehension is often more painful than the evil dreaded. When the misfortune comes, we see what it is, we measure it, we touch its limits. But from a distance, imagination magnifies it, lends it frightful shapes and aspects. Nothing is more agonizing than to feel the shadow of an inevitable sorrow drawing nearer every instant. God is good, therefore, to drop an impenetrable curtain between the present moment and the following one, for, if we knew what the future has in store for us, we could not live, or at least we would live in perpetual anxiety.

This curtain was partly drawn in Mary's case. When she took the divine Child on her knees, when she changed or adjusted the swaddling-bands, she thought, perhaps, of the day when she would bury Him. Already she saw in His Hands, in His Feet, ghastly wounds, and on His Head a crown, in no way like a royal diadem. Then her embrace would become closer, more tender, as though to

67

safe-guard Him, or to compensate Him in advance for His future Passion.

If, about A.D.1900, the mother of a family had been told: "Madam, in fifteen years from now this little boy, playing here under your eyes, will be torn to pieces by a bomb, and agonize on a battlefield with no one to help him," what superhuman courage that woman would have required to master her grief and carry on her mission of education and training in spite of it! Mary's case was somewhat similar. She knew that the life of her Jesus would be but a cross and a martyrdom. Nevertheless, she preserved her serenity. The depths of her soul were stirred by suffering, but the surface remained unruffled. During her whole life, which was a way of the cross, her courage never faltered, for she was sustained by her faith and her piety. Those who have no other will than the Will of God, those who have Mary's *Fiat* ever on their lips are far more imperturbable than the ancient Stoics; they are upheld, not by pride, but by love; they rely, not on themselves, but on God.

And the Child Jesus, did He foresee His destiny? Did He know that He would have to suffer before entering into His Glory? Assuredly: His soul united to the divinity was flooded with light. Of the marvels within Him, He allowed nothing to appear. Apparently He was growing and developing like other children of His age; but beneath this humble exterior He hid thoughts and sentiments more than human. During His sleep when Mary gazed on the closed eyelids, on His little lips half-open, and listened to His soft, regular breathing, she may have said to herself: "Perhaps He is dreaming of the ransom He will have to pay for the salvation of the world."

O my Saviour, You once said: "Be not solicitous for the morrow; sufficient for the day is the evil thereof." That is true, but we can not help looking out for the future. What has it in store for us? a new persecution? a new revolution? a new war? The anxious world is restless, in search of an equilibrium nowhere to be found, and in its tossings and convulsions, it crushes many an innocent being. What reassures us is that nothing will happen to us that has not been foreseen and ordained by a Will solicitous for our sanctification and salvation. The more we penetrate ourselves with this thought, the more peaceful we shall be.

> To will what God wills is the great science
> That keeps us at rest.

X

The Poetry of Nazareth

Nazareth is a sanctuary where God dwells. To form any idea of its charm, of its poetry, we have only to compare it to our churches.

In the Tabernacle Jesus is in hiding. He is enclosed in a ciborium and the appearances of bread are like the white robe that covers His humanity.

At Nazareth this sacred humanity appears, but itself hides the divinity. To the eyes of His compatriots, Jesus is the "son of the carpenter". Exteriorly there is nothing to distinguish Him from the other lads of His age. He dresses like the others, He follows the customs of the country. On the Sabbath, He goes to the synagogue. Lost in the crowd, He listens to the ancients, who, after reading a passage of Scripture, comment upon it as best they can. Among these venerable men, who were expecting the coming of the Messias, not one suspected that He was there, under their very eyes, concealed beneath the garments of a young workman.

What also strikes us in our churches, especially during the afternoon hours, is their silence.

> . . . All-enveloping and magnificent, this silence
> In purity seems a harmonious portico,
> Opening to the beauty of the world within.

Absolute silence is always impressive: the silence of closed chambers, where specks of dust dance in the sunbeam slanting through a chink; the silence of the vast forest undisturbed by the flight of a midge; the silence of the countryside, asleep in the moonlight. However, in our chambers, our forests, our countryside, we are surrounded only by things that are by nature mute. In the church we are in the presence of the living God. And when we think that the voice that healed so many sick, that called back to life so many dead, has been silent for centuries under outrages and blasphemies, we can not help shuddering, and Pascal's words come to mind: "The eternal silence of the infinite terrifies me."

At Nazareth, the same silence. Jesus rarely exchanges a word with His Mother. Why should they converse when they understand each other so perfectly? To those who love, a glance, a smile, say more than much talk.

> The heart, in deepest silence,
> Can proffer the infinite.

For all that, this prolonged silence amazes us. Jesus has the gift of swaying the crowd, He could hold them for hours by the charm of His words, whole days even they hung upon His lips. And He is silent, . . . He knows secrets that would transform the world, and He keeps them to Himself. He holds Himself in reserve, He awaits His hour. Silence full of promises, in which one feels the palpitation of a divine mystery!

When one comes from the hub-bub of a busy street into a church, it is a relief to find stillness and peace there. Outside is feverish excitement. The passers-by hurry, there is pushing and jostling, they are rushing to their business or to their pleasure. They hardly exchange a glance as they pass each other. Our century calls the whirl by which we get from one place to another "progress"; those who go fastest are the idle, for they, more than any others, feel the need to divert their thoughts.

But within the church, what calm, what recollection! No stir, save the flame of the sanctuary lamp, whose flicker seems praying for those who do not pray. This peace, sensible, palpable, acts on the restless souls that allow it to sink into them, and for a delicious moment it relieves them from their worries.

Nazareth also is the home of peace. The members of the Holy Family live in perfect harmony, for they love God with all their mind, with all their heart, with all their strength. Their thoughts take flight together and following converging lines, rejoin each other in the infinite, above. God, whom one of our moralists so justly calls the "*place*" of souls, is also their *bond*.

The Sacred Host appears inert. And nevertheless, what activity, how it radiates vitality! From His tabernacle, Jesus follows us with His eyes. He awaits our visits, He offers us the life that He received in the bosom of His Father and that He wishes to communicate to us. He preaches by example, and the ciborium in which He rests is a silent school of the loftiest virtues. He never ceases performing acts of religion: He adores, He gives thanks, and to obtain pardon for us, He offers His infinite merits. The Divine Lamb is always in a state of immolation, and it is by this ever-renewed, uninterrupted sacrifice that He saves the world. Where could Almighty justice strike us down, since the whole earth is white with Hosts?

In Nazareth, Jesus obeyed, He worked with His Hands. He set an example of the humble virtues which most men have to practice in the humble sphere in which they live. He offered His weariness, His suffering, for the salvation of humanity. He prepared Himself in seclusion for His future mission. Thus in the winter, a lily-bulb, hidden in the earth, seems dead; but it is storing up sap, gathering strength, pulling itself together, as it were, for the spring flowering.

And how many virtues, what sanctity, in the humble house of Nazareth! the poverty of the setting but throws into higher relief the moral nobility of the personages.

How could one possibly not admire that workman, so generous, so modest, devoting himself constantly to the service of the Divine Child and effacing himself as soon as his presence is no longer necessary?

Lovelier still is his young companion. Her grace is so radiant that it envelops all that surrounds her.

The air that she has breathed retains the taste of Heaven,
And where her foot has trod, the earth still smiles.

And yet this beauty is but a reflection, a participation. It was with a view to Christ that the Most-High formed Mary. She is the dawn of a radiant day. Jesus is beauty itself. Those who see Him, . . . if they are pure, . . . feel drawn to Him; and the Angels, who know Him better than men can, are never weary of contemplating Him.

This beauty is mysterious, which doubles its charm. When we know all about a person, when there is nothing more to rouse our interest, or call for our appreciation, our love can not increase. It rather tends to decrease, like all emotions that are prolonged. But Jesus is a treasure of which we can never make a complete inventory. In Him dwells the plenitude of the Divinity; that is to say, an infinity of infinite attributes.

A child who had been told that the starry vault above is but the wrong side of Heaven, exclaimed ingenuously: "Since the wrong side of Heaven is so splendid, Mother, how wonderful the other side must be!" That child was a poet; behind the appearances he sensed a more beautiful reality.

This presentiment is often deceptive. When, gazing on the setting sun, I think I see the walls and domes of a fairy city, I know that the city exists only in my imagination. It is a mirage, a symbol of the perfect happiness I vainly seek here below.

But in Jesus there is no disappointment to fear. Study Him as we may, we shall never reach the end of our study, for He perpetually opens out to our ardor new infinities. Expand our concepts as we will, we shall for ever remain below the divine reality. Jesus resembles the Temple of Jerusalem, where, after traversing the Court of the Gentiles, the Court of the Hebrews and penetrated into the Sanctuary, one came to the Holy of Holies whose splendor no human eye save the High-Priest's had ever admired.

Nazareth is more than a Paradise. What is Heaven, if not the vision, the possession of God? If for an instant Jesus lifted the veil which hides His Divinity from our eyes, it would be Heaven for us, and the poverty of the setting would vanish in the dazzling brilliance of the divine beauty.

And you, pious soul, are you not another Nazareth? When you go to Holy Communion, you become a living tabernacle. As long as you remain in the state of grace, you are a sanctuary in which the adorable Trinity resides. O be proud of your distinction! Be as pure and shining as a temple of marble and gold, where there is nothing to displease the divine eye. Let yourself be penetrated by this glance, which purifies, consoles, strengthens, and while enjoying your present dignity, live in expectation of a yet more blissful Heaven.

XI

THE LIVING OSTENSORIUM

A FAMOUS painting by Raphael, called The Virgin of the Blue Diadem, hangs in the Louvre. The Infant Jesus is asleep on a cushion, in a graceful attitude of relaxation. Mary, kneeling beside Him, lifts with one hand the veil that covers Him and lays the other on St. John's shoulder, as if to say: "See how beautiful He is! Adore Him, love Him!"

The artist has well symbolized one of the most glorious functions of the Blessed Virgin. When the Magi arrived in Bethlehem, upon what throne did they find the King of Israel seated? It was upon Mary's knee; and it is easy to imagine with what grace, what noble simplicity, what dignity she performed the office of living ostensorium. And when she passed through the streets of Nazareth carrying the Divine Child in her arms, she was the first Corpus Christi procession, since she was showing to men the Word Incarnate.

She showed Him also (in a different way) in her features, in her character, in her life. God had adorned her with the gifts and virtues which were to shine forth so brilliantly in Jesus. As time went on she became the first and most perfect of His disciples. She steeped herself in His thoughts, His spirit, she was His living image.

We are told that the first Christians used to undertake long journeys to see the Apostle St. James the Less, because of His resemblance to Jesus, his cousin according to the flesh. But in Mary this likeness was still more striking. When the Apostles wanted to recall the outward appearance of their Master, they needed but to look at His Mother.

In the course of centuries, Mary has continued her rôle of "Monstrance". See, for instance, what has happened at Lourdes. The first pilgrims, doubtless, thought only of paying homage to the Immaculate Virgin who had deigned to converse with a shephardess of the Pyrenees. But little by little, devotion took another course. Miracles no longer took place only in the piscina or in front of the Grotto, but on the broad terrace, during the procession of the Blessed Sacrament. It seems that the Virgin draws the faithful thither in order to lead them to her divine Son.

Even in heaven, she will show Jesus to us and present us to Him. The author of the Salve Regina says explicitly: "Et Jesum, benedictum fructum ventris tui, *nobis post hoc exilium ostende."* This belief rests on solid doctrine. Mary was the intermediary through whom the Heavenly Father gave us His Son. He gave Him in the Crib as Companion, in the Cenacle as Food, on Calvary, as Victim, and He will give Him to us in Heaven as Reward. Mary collaborated with Him in the first three mysteries. Without her, there would have been no Incarnation, He Whom we receive at the Sacred Banquet was formed in her virginal womb. By uniting her sufferings with His, she has deserved the glorious title of Co-Redemptress of the human race. It is just, therefore, that the divine Work should be completed with her; All through Mary . . . even Heaven! *Omnis nos voluit habere per Mariam!*

Christian artists love to represent Mary in her functions of Ostensorium. At Brébières, for instance, she is lifting up the Divine Child at arm's length, while He Himself offers us a Cross. "Look," she seems to say, "look at this innocent Victim. It is by His Cross that you will be saved."

Like Mary, the Christian must be not only a ciborium but also an ostensorium. He must be so penetrated with the Eucharistic Spirit that it will shine out without his being aware of it, in his speech, in his conduct, in his whole person.

Believers sometimes say things which sound a false note on their lips. When success or some unexpected legacy lifts a person from poverty to wealth, they exclaim: "That's a lucky fellow!" Instead of congratulating him, would they not do better to fear, or still better, to pray for him? Looked at from the supernatural point of view, it is easily seen that the *sudden* acquisition of wealth is a grave danger.

In like vein, when some one dies after a long, painful illness, these demi-Christians say: "Her sufferings are over! What a happy deliverance for her!" Is death the cessation of existence? Does it mean for everyone and immediately the bliss of paradise? These examples show that in some cases Christian ideas are relegated to certain compartments in the mind. They are not cast aside, but they are not used. Such persons do not radiate Christ.

It is not opportune, of course, to parade one's faith and piety. If its manifestation is liable to provoke irritating arguments, disputes, sarcasms, blasphemies, without profit to anyone, it is wiser to refrain. But prudence is one thing and betrayal is another. Those who go to Mass and judge things according to worldly standards are practically denying their Faith.

Here we are touching upon one of the weaknesses of our times. Why is it that so many Catholics have so little influence? Because, outside the walls of the church, their principle is to do like everyone else. In their social intercourse, in their ordinary conversations, nothing distinguishes them from the rest. It would seem, however, that if we expect a native of Italy to speak Italian, we should with more reason expect a disciple of Christ to use Christian speech. Since the Lord is in his heart, He should be also on his lips.

And, we may add, *in his conduct.*—In any given situation two reactions are possible: the natural reaction (the reaction of nature), and the Christian reaction (the reaction of grace). When misfortune befalls, how many fly into a passion, rage, blaspheme? They blame Providence for all the disasters, all the disagreeables that happen to them. Others kiss their cross instead of trying to break it. The gesture is more Christian and more beautiful.

When we are ridiculed, insulted, our first impulse is to return contempt for contempt, jibe for jibe. But let us think of Christ on the Cross, and we shall maintain our self-control, the calmness and the dignity which befit the children of God. We shall pity those who abuse us, for they harm no one but themselves.

Let us imitate, so far as we can, Father Pro-Juarez, S.J., one of the victims of the odious Mexican persecution.

The Mother of Jesus

He had returned from Europe where he had made his
theological studies. Captured, condemned to death and
led to the place of execution, he absolutely refused to be
blindfolded, he looked straight at the firing-squad, and to
these men, about to kill him, the 26-year-old priest gave
his last blessing.

The priest is said to be another Christ. If the witnesses
of this scene had still a remnant of faith, did they not see
in Father Pro, a living portrait of Jesus Crucified?

The Evangelical spirit finally must shine forth *from
our whole person*. When one dear to us is indisposed or
fatigued, he does not have to tell us so. We see it in
his pallor, the circles under his eyes, etc. If our physical
condition is so obvious why does not our spiritual state, our
Christian spirit, manifest itself exteriorly? In those permeated thoroughly with it, it does. There is something in
the voice, in the look, in their smile, that is quite distinctive. It is a charm that does not emanate from themselves.
They diffuse around them the good odor of Jesus Christ.
How true was the remark of a pilgrim returning from
Ars: "I have seen God in a man!"

Every Christian who has no mortal sin on his soul is a
temple in which God dwells. But the walls of this sanctuary are not always transparent. What renders them

impermeable to light is venial sin, lack of generosity, resistance to grace; these stains prevent the divine Guest of their souls from being seen. They are God-*Bearers,* but not God-*Revealers.* They bear God within, they do not manifest Him without. They are Ciboria not Ostensoria.

Purify me, O Lord, from attachment to sin, from sensuality, from egotism. May I become a clear crystal through which You may be seen and attract souls! If nothing but the man can be perceived in me, I shall do no good. I must efface myself in order that You may act.

XII

THE EDUCATRESS OF JESUS

HAD Jesus any need to be educated? Evidently not, since He had attained from the beginning the peak of human perfection. His soul, united to the Divinity, was enriched from the first by all supernatural gifts, all the virtues. From the first instant of His conception, He possessed the most eminent sanctity. According to St. John's expression in his admirable Prologue, He was "full of grace."

But as He wished to resemble His brethren in all things, He manifested only partially and progressively the spiritual treasures He possessed, so that His intellectual and moral development seemed to follow that of His body. His life was a continual "Epiphany" for which His Mother's lessons provided the occasion. Since she had formed His body, it was her place to form also His soul. This honor belonged to her by right.

It was she who taught Him to speak. Aramaic, the first language in which the Gospel was drawn up, was the mother-tongue of Jesus. The Child learned from His Mother not only words, expressions, modes of speech, but the provincial accent, familiar gestures, idioms, etc. In the style and diction of the divine Preacher, there was, therefore, something of Mary, the reflection of her teachings.

It was she also who taught Him to walk. One loves to imagine the Blessed Virgin holding Him up as He tries His first steps. Then she places Him at a little distance from her and calls Him to her. Jesus hesitates, He has never yet walked alone. At last, He tries, He ventures to cross the distance, totters, recovers His balance, then trembling and smiling, He throws Himself into His Mother's arms.

It is a lovely scene that it is good to ponder, for it helps us to a better understanding of St. Paul's words: *Exinanivit semetipsum.* The Son of God annihilated Himself voluntarily for love of us. He Whom the Angels adore, stripped off His glory. He Whose immensity fills the universe, shrank in some incomprehensible way into the body of an Infant. He, the Omnipotent, walks, stumbles, held up by a woman's hand!

St. Luke tells us that in the Temple of Jerusalem the boy, Jesus, questioned the Doctors. Why did He question them, since He foreknew their answers? At twelve years of age He possessed an innate or infused knowledge incomparably superior to that of the greatest theologians. But in order not to reveal it before the time, He allowed Himself to be instructed. What He already knew, He wished to learn.

He must also have put to His Mother those "Hows?" and "Whys?" that come so quickly to children's lips as soon as their minds begin to work. Mary replied with her upright judgment, her sound good sense; and He admired interiorly the agreement of human reason with divine intellect. The Word is the uncreated light that enlightens every man that comes into this world. When we follow this light, when our interior eye is not dimmed either by self-interest or the passions, we see the Truth, i.e. we think the thoughts of God.

Parents are sometimes obliged to reprove their children: Baptism, which restrains concupiscence, does not entirely destroy it. It remains at the bottom of the purest souls like slime at the bottom of a limpid pool. Occasionally this mud rises to the surface. Even in children who have not reached the age of reason traces of almost all the capital sins can be observed: pride, jealousy, gluttony, anger, sloth. They must therefore be corrected early, trained and drilled, until their conscience awakes and they are capable of being taught moral lessons.

86

Let us hasten to add that the work of correction never fell to Mary's lot. Every one acts as he is, according to the axiom, "as a thing *is,* so it acts". The human nature of Jesus being perfectly sound, all His acts were good. In His conduct there was neither excess nor defect. He did all things well. This regular life, always and in every respect conformed to duty, is like a limpid brook, flowing over a bed of sparkling sand between flowery banks.

All Christian parents should have constantly before their eyes Mary's example as educatress. Is it not their mission to form Jesus in their children?

Baptism is not simply an ablution which purifies by effacing original sin. It bestows the right to the Beatific Vision, the aptitude to know God as He knows Himself; in other words, it confers a participation in the divine nature. God adopts the baptized soul as His child; He raises it to the dignity of brother and co-heir of Christ. This is so true, that baptized children who die before the age of reason go straight to heaven.

But of adults God requires more. Since they are His children, they must behave as such, imitate the Word-made-Flesh, the Man par excellence,—think, feel, act, like Him. The Father loves His Son, and also those who resemble Him. We shall not be admitted to Heaven unless we bear, with the Baptismal mark, the image and inscription of Christ.

Taken as a whole, the faithful engrafted on Christ, may be compared to an immense tree. "I am the vine, you are the branches," said Jesus Himself. But the cells of an organism are not merely in juxtaposition, they are not aggregations, they are assimilations.

This work of assimilation is accomplished in part by Christ Who begins and sustains our supernatural life. "It is Thou, Lord Jesus," said St. Augustine, "yes, it is Thou, Who, with a most gentle and merciful, yet most firm Hand, dost work and shape my heart." There is not a moment when Christ, living in us, is not enlightening our mind, touching our heart, strengthening our will. But this incessant work of grace calls for our co-operation. Christ might say to us: "Not you, without Me; not I, without you."

As long as children are incapable of grasping these great truths, while their will is still weak and inconstant, it is the parents' task to mould them to the likeness of Jesus. They must labor with them until the Christ be formed in them.

If parents realize and take to heart the greatness of their mission, they will follow the counsel of an ancient moralist: *Maxima debetur puero reverentia.*

We do, indeed, owe the greatest respect, nay, "reverence" to the child. He is not an idol for adulation, not a doll to be dressed and caparisoned, not a graceful little animal whose frolicsome gambols are to be watched with amused interest or curiosity.

> Take care of this small being, O take care!
> He's great,—he contains God! Beware! Beware! [1]

Issuing from the Baptismal Font, the child possesses the life of grace, the divine life which will one day blossom into glory.

Full of respect for the sacredness of this little one, parents will be careful not to scandalize him. There are some who discuss all sorts of things before small children under the pretext that they do not understand. How do they know? Intelligence dawns sometimes sooner than one expects. And even if children do not understand the sense of the words, they can remember them, think about them, understand them before the right time. These premature revelations can not but tarnish the childish soul. That is why Jesus threatens severe chastisement to those who scandalize the little ones who believe in Him. St. Paul, on his side, says: "Woe to him who destroyeth the Temple of God, for him shall God destroy!"

[1] Victor Hugo.

Christian parents should also endeavor to develop the love of God in their children. Of what use is it to give counsels to those who have not the courage to follow them? Now the great motive of spiritual life is charity. *Ama, et fac quod vis!* said St. Augustine. Love God above all things, love Him entirely, ardently, and you will develop a strong and upright will. You will discern clearly the path to follow and you will step out upon it fearlessly. *Ubi amatur, non laboratur,* adds the great Doctor. When one loves, one does not suffer; or, if one does suffer, one loves the suffering.

When the parents' mission is accomplished, when their children are no longer under their tutelage, the work of configuration with Christ is not yet complete. It is the duty of each individual to carry on the work, for fear,— and the fear is alas! but too justified—that it will not be completed, . . . at least, not in this life. Every picture of Jesus is a disappointment; what a discrepancy between these material portraits and the ideal we have formed in our minds! Every one of the faithful should be a living portrait of Christ; is there no discrepancy between the original and the copy? between what we should be and what we really are? Is it not undeniable?

No discouragement, though! Let us never lose sight of

our divine Model, even be it only to humble ourselves and to stir ourselves up to better work. Let us rectify the errors, push on nearer and nearer to our ideal, and if we find ourselves without either courage or generosity, let us have sincerity of heart at least!

O Mary, model of educators, help us in this task so necessary, but so painful and so long drawn out! Take from us all that offends your eyes, . . . efface everything in us that still savors of the pagan, . . . that is too human! Make us like to Jesus!

XIII

He Grew

"Jesus grew in age and in wisdom before God and before men." These words which the Evangelist applies to the divine adolescent, are more appropriate to His first childhood. It is in the beginning of life that development is most rapid. Then it is that take place in quick succession those transformations that delight mothers and amaze the observer.

> At ev'ry step He takes, with ev'ry act,
> The Child a tiny phantom leaves behind,
> As though life sought, with charming, gracious tact,
> To try on Him halos of ev'ry kind.[1]

Speaking to a predestined child, whom some regarded as a figure of the Saviour, Virgil said:

> *Incipe, parve puer, risu cognoscere matrem.*[2]

Before he has learned to speak, the child knows how to smile, and what charm in that first smile by which

[1] Victor Hugo.
[2] Eclogues, IV.

he "recognizes his mother" and which attests the simultaneous awakening of his intelligence and his heart!

What joy then for the Virgin-Mother when she received the first caress of Jesus, when for the first time He stammered that sweet word "Mother", that word of tenderness and confidence, word of abandonment of the God-made-Man to her who was His visible Providence.

Mary knew the value of the treasure that she possessed. The Archangel had said to her: "The Holy that shall be born of thee, shall be called the Son of the Most-High". When He was born, she made an act of faith in His Divinity. She adored the new-born Babe, frail and crying, Whose eyes seemed to be fixed upon her. But as time went on her faith was more and more confirmed, as the Divine Soul began to blossom. She went from discovery to discovery, from surprise to surprise. The life of Jesus was an incessant revelation for her. Our wonder would be less if a star, approaching us, displayed against the vault of heaven the marvels it contains.

A poet said to his lady-love:

I listen to the universe in thee, . . .
Forspent, enthralled from plundering thy heart, . . .
From thee, as from a treasury, I draw forth
Thy very self; nay, more, . . . with reverent touch
I waken, in thy depths, the sleeping God! [1]

[1] P. Géraldy.

Beautiful words, but perhaps inspired by passion, that teacher of error and falsehood. It happens sometimes that we idealize our friends and deck them with imaginary qualities. But applied to the infancy of Jesus these words are replete with a meaning that enchants us. It is true to say that in Jesus a God slumbers, or rather, hides. He manifests Himself little by little, and it is Mary who is, I do not say the cause, but the occasion, of this never-ending epiphany. With what loving attention, what ever-watchful curiosity she bent over the budding soul whose flower was gradually opening and softly wafting its perfume to her!

Every mother wants her son, while resembling her, to be more perfect, more powerful, more fortunate than she. This wish of Mary's was so completely granted that it made her companions jealous. Witness the woman who cried out one day when Jesus was speaking to the multitudes: "Blessed is the womb that bore thee and the breast that gave thee suck!" This joy that was hers in its plenitude only during His public life, she knew by foretaste during the years of His childhood. Admiring her Son's grace, the perfection with which He did everything, she wondered, like the relatives and friends of Zachary, astonished at the portents that accompanied the birth of the Precursor: "What shall this Child be?" In all His words, in all His actions, she saw a presage of His future glory.

One should not fancy, however, that His life was a continual ecstasy. Mary was not congealed in an attitude of veneration. The God-Man wished to resemble His brethren in all respects. During His first years, He laughed and played like children of His age, and Mary, carrying Him in her arms, never leaving Him a single instant, joined in His innocent mirth.

She blossomed out in Him. A mother is so identified with her child that she is humbled by his blunders and proud of his success. Even if she remains in poverty and obscurity, she feels herself uplifted when her son achieves wealth or fame. Thus Mary grew with Him Who was her double, the flesh of her flesh. Every progress made by Jesus was a gain for her.

When the acorn, buried in the earth, begins to sprout, the oak contained within it begins to develop. It already exists virtually. According to the comparison in the Gospel, the Church is a great tree that covers the earth with its spreading branches. With its doctrine, its institutions, its hierarchy, it seems to us an extremely complex organism. But before it had become so wide-spread, it was contained in germ in the soul of its Founder. In bringing Jesus up, therefore, Mary was also bringing up the Church. Such is the power of a mother; the hand that rocks the cradle, moves the world.

The Mother of Jesus

What we did, what we said at the age of three or four years, we have completely forgotten. An impenetrable night shrouds our first years. But our mothers' recollections supply what our memory can not tell us. Simple incidents told us by them enable us to relive our years of happy unconsciousness.

Thus the Blessed Virgin kept and pondered in her heart the facts she had witnessed. It was from her, they say, that St. Luke obtained the information which he has preserved in his Gospel, called the Gospel of the Infancy. But what is this picture, however charming, beside what Mary kept to herself! On the day of her Assumption, she carried it to Heaven with her. There we shall see it; there we shall contemplate, with unutterable rapture, the scenes of the Divine Infancy!

But it is good for us to think about them now, as far as our incapacity permits, in order to understand better those inspired words: "The Word was made flesh, and dwelt amongst us . . . He annihilated Himself." Better than any general considerations, what gives an idea of this prodigious annihilation is to watch the divine Child shaping His lips in imitation of His Mother's for His first words.

He Who knew all things, deigned to learn. He, perfection itself, develops like the imperfect beings we are. On

96

the eve of His Passion, He said concerning His disciples: *Propter eos sanctifico meipsum* . . . "For them I *sacrifice* Myself". But let us read what follows: *Ut ipsi sint sanctificati in veritate.* Here there is question of the disciples' progress in virtue and piety. Now the same verb can not have two meanings in the same sentence. We must therefore translate: "For them I *sanctify* Myself". Doubtless, from the first instant of His conception, Jesus possessed the plenitude of grace. But he did not exhibit at once the whole treasure that was in Him. If the Sun of Justice had blazed forth in full splendor, it would have dazzled us. He concealed Himself behind a cloud, and disclosed Himself only little by little. The Gospel says with a clearness that leaves no room for doubt: "The Child grew in wisdom."

His example invites us to grow continually. When we have reached the age of twenty-five or thirty, they say of us: He is a grown man. Alas! the grown man is frequently in need of repairs or of completion! Never shall we attain our ideal, which is the Christ. Hasten as we may, when we have reached the end of life, we shall still find much to be done; and like the farmer of whom Virgil speaks, we shall have to leave the plough in the middle of the furrow.

Let us then follow St. Augustine's advice: *Semper tibi displiceat quod es; semper profice, semper ambula, semper adde.* "Never be satisfied with what you are, always go forward, always press on, always increase."

We must grow, because we have not yet used all our talents, or, to speak in modern parlance, realized on our potentialities. Matter, they say, is a condensation of energy. In a pebble on the road, there is force enough to drive a locomotive some miles. A gram of radium emits in one minute millions of millions of corpuscles, and this bombardment goes on for half a century without any loss of weight or activity in the mass. But how speak of the potentialities of souls? To form an idea of their power, think of Jeanne d'Arc, the Curé d'Ars, Thérèse of Lisieux. These souls diffused in their life-time and are still diffusing floods of light over the wide world. And how? Because they gave all that was in them, because they loved much.

Alas! such absolute generosity is rare. How many resemble strong-boxes, full of valuables never used. The key is lost, or the owner does not wish to use it. He lives for himself, not for souls or for God.

One day when Guynemer had fought three battles in the air, and announced that he was off again, his comrades said to him: "Are you crazy?" The young hero replied:

"Until a man has given everything, he has given nothing!"

My God, grant that I may understand and above all put in practice these heroic words! During the time I still have to live, . . . how many years? . . . how many months? . . . may I use in Your service all that I have and all that I am. Dispose of my time, of my strength, of all my resources.

"Teach me to be generous, to give without counting the cost, to fight without minding the wounds, to work without seeking rest, to spend myself without expecting any reward but that of knowing that I am doing Your Holy Will." [1]

[1] Prayer of the French Scouts.

XIV

Jesus at Ten Years of Age

"From April on, fruits are what they will be later," says the proverb. The man is heralded by the child. Country, climate, education have a considerable influence on the formation of mind and character.

Although He was God, and consequently Master of Himself and of all things, Jesus willed as man, to subject Himself to the common law. Many traits of His moral conduct can not be explained without recalling the kind of life He had led in His childhood.

Let us represent to ourselves the Divine Child at the age of ten. He is dressed according to the custom of the country, in a striped tunic. His hair, untouched by the shears, falls in ringlets over His shoulders. His face, tanned by the sun of the Orient, expresses extraordinary intelligence and precocious maturity. It costs an effort to turn one's eyes from Him. One feels a mystery about Him which commands respect.

His days are very full. He goes to the school held in the synagogue, a rectangular hall, furnished with benches for the pupils, a pulpit for the master, and a coffer, in which are kept the books of Holy Writ. The children, under the direction of the Hazzan, or usual Reader, are drilled in reading, and in writing the beautiful Hebrew characters. They must also learn by heart the verses of the Bible which begin with the letters of their own name. In a word, their formation is wholly moral and religious.

In the intervals between classes, Jesus plays with His companions. To imagine Him always solemn and majestic would be to form a very false notion of Him. He wished to resemble His brethren in all things. He Who loved to call Himself "the Son of Man" took part, therefore, in the games of children of His age, to which He alludes in the Gospel, several of which, such as huckle-bones and hop-scotch are still played by our school-boys.

The formation at school was completed by the lessons and example of family life, especially prayer in common. It was customary among the Jews to pray three times a day. We like to think of the Holy Family praying in the evening on a terrace bright with anemones. The sinking sun darts a golden beam over the whiteness of the houses. From the valley below Nazareth, called by the ancients "the valley of flowers", rise aromatic perfumes. On every path is heard the trotting of flocks and herds, returning from the pastures or the mountain. But heedless of all these sights and sounds, so familiar to them, and absorbed in prayer, Jesus and Mary, hand in hand, gaze upward to Heaven. They watch the first stars come out, and think of the house of the Heavenly Father, of that blissful Kingdom whence Jesus has come down to reveal its existence and point out the way to it.

These details known, make it easier to grasp certain incidents in His life and certain traits of character in Jesus.

Notice first of all that He has always lived among the people. His first companions were the sons of workmen and peasants, that is, tillers of the soil. Hence His preference for the humble. Hence also, the simplicity and familiarity of His teaching. It might seem that the sublimity of His divine nature, the depth of His intelligence, should have dug an impassable gulf between Him and His disciples. But it is nothing of the sort. Jesus is on the same footing as His hearers; He makes no effort to adapt Himself to them. He does not need to condescend, to lower Himself in order to be understood; He has only to speak the language He has spoken from babyhood.

The same reasons enable us to comprehend His fondness for comparisons drawn from domestic life. He says, for instance, not to hide the lamp under a bushel-basket, not to sew a piece of new cloth as a patch on an old garment, not to put new wine into old skins. Elsewhere He compares the Christian spirit to leaven, which a woman puts into three measures of flour to make the dough rise. To illustrate the joy which the return of a sinner gives to God, He tells of the housekeeper, who, having lost a groat, lights her lamp and sweeps the house, and when she has found it, calls in her friends and neighbors to share her joy. Who knows whether this picturesque scene may not be a childish recollection? A coin meant something valuable to the Holy Family, perhaps their whole wealth. What a dismay, then, if it were lost! and what relief, when after long and thorough search, it was at last recovered!

Again, how many times, with the natural curiosity of childhood, did not Jesus watch His mother take three measures of flour, one for each member of the Holy Family, and knead the leaven into it with her delicate hands? How many times did He not see Joseph prune the vine, or cut down a fig-tree, which took up a great deal of space in the family garden without bearing fruit! His lively imagination saw at once the relation of these trifling incidents of domestic life to religious truths. Later on He was to say to His disciples: "The Heavenly Father is trying you. He is pruning you, so that you may bear more fruit. Bring forth the fruit of good works. Every barren tree shall be cut down and cast into the fire."

The early formation of Jesus also accounts for His frequest allusions to the Old Testament. The Bible was His favorite book, or rather, His only one. He recognizes Himself on every page of this divine Book, which is full of Him. Between the events in the History of Israel and His own story, He recognizes striking analogies.

In the Brazen Serpent set up in the desert by Moses, which cured all those bitten by the asps if they but looked at it, He saw a figure of His Passion. One day He also would be raised upon a Cross, and those who gazed upon Him with confidence would be cured of the venomous bites of the infernal serpent.

Like Jonas, He will remain three days in darkness and immobility, but on the third day, death will give back its prey.

Jesus knows that the Psalmist has sung of Him. The Psalm *Dixit Dominus,* which we sing at Vespers on Sunday, paints His portrait. It speaks of a Messias, begotten by God from all eternity and seated at His right hand. This Messias will tread His enemies under foot and reign over the whole earth. He shall be a priest according to the order of Melchisedech; instead of bloody victims, He will offer in sacrifice bread and wine. This Psalm which we sing so often, Jesus sang before us, either in the Synagogue of Nazareth or in the Temple of Jerusalem; and what must have been His emotion to see that ten centuries earlier, David, His ancestor according to the flesh, had depicted Him with such fidelity!

How His adorable Heart must have quickened when, seated near His Mother in the evening recollection, He read the celebrated passage in Isaias: "Behold a Virgin shall conceive and bring forth a Son, and his name shall be called Emmanuel." What for the ancient prophet was but a distant apparition, was for Jesus an august and sublime reality.

Ezechiel, speaking of the princes and pontiffs of Juda, calls them wicked shepherds: "The weak you have not strengthened, and that which was sick, you have not healed, . . . that which was driven away, you have not brought again, neither have you sought that which was lost, . . . the shepherds fed themselves and fed not my sheep, . . . Therefore, ye shepherds, hear the word of the Lord: Behold, I myself come upon the shepherds, and I will cause them to cease from feeding the flock any more, . . . Behold, I myself will seek my sheep and will visit them . . ." (Ezechiel, Chap. 34).

One day He will Himself be the Shepherd of His people. Jesus has this allegory in mind when He compares

Himself to the Good Shepherd who defends His flock from the wolf, and brings back on His shoulders the lost sheep.

Before Caiaphas He will recall that passage in Daniel which says that the Son of Man will come in the clouds of heaven with great power and majesty. Thus the whole substance of the Bible, so constantly read in His childhood, passed into His teaching.

Let us no longer be surprised after this that He deigned to pass so long a period of His life at Nazareth. Thirty years of obscurity against three years of public life! Why did He not reveal Himself sooner, at twenty, for instance, when He was in the bloom of youth? Why did He hide His light so long under a bushel?

Those who ask such childish questions forget that divine wisdom infinitely surpasses ours. All God does is well done. If Jesus remained hidden for thirty years, He had good reasons for doing so. The majority of mankind lives in a humble, dependent condition. As the model of all, He wished to give the working class an example of resignation to God's Will, and to teach them how to sanctify their labor.

He also wished to remind those who work to spread the Gospel, of the necessity of preparation for their apostolate.

Apostles can not be improvised. They must give of their own fulness. If a man wishes to communicate to others, faith, hope of a future life, love of Christ, he himself must possess those virtues in a high degree. During the long years of probation, in noviceship or seminary, he must store up in himself, as in a deep well, not only clear, definite ideas, but sincere stimulating sentiments, which the slightest touch will release to gush forth as from an inexhaustible spring.

The example of Jesus is not merely a lesson for us, but a consolation as well. We all lead a hidden life more or less. We are sometimes crossed in our most cherished aspirations. Which of us is as pious, as pure, as charitable as he would like to be? Which of us has done all the good that he should have done? which of us has fully realized the glowing dreams of his adolescence? By a sort of fatality, and despite all our efforts, this life is made up of disappointments. Let us not lose confidence, however. Our present life is but a rough sketch, but a prelude of a better one. Here below we vegetate, like a blade of grass that dwindles and pines and loses all color beneath a stone. But one day God will remove all the obstacles which now thwart our development. After Nazareth will come Thabor. After this obscure and frustrated life, will come its full flowering in light and joy.

XV

The Child Jesus at Jacob's Well

At twelve years of age, Jesus for the first time made the pilgrimage to Jerusalem. The Galilean caravans sometimes passed through Samaria and halted at the watering-place. It is, therefore, probable that the Holy Family may have joined a group that stopped near Jacob's Well, within sight of Sichar.

Let us imagine the scene, at once picturesque and suggestive. While the men are unloading the beasts of burden, setting up the tents, kindling fires for the evening meal, the women go to draw water in the water-skins. Jesus accompanies His Mother. He, for Whom the future holds no secrets, thinks of the Samaritan woman whom He will meet here later and the interview that He will have with her is already present to His mind.

The sun, about to set, lights up with its last rays the imposing mass of Mount Garizim. It was there that the Samaritans had erected their Temple. They wanted a

108

priesthood, a worship of their own, and for that reason
were despised, detested and excommunicated by the Jews
who contended that outside the Temple of Jerusalem
no one had a right to offer sacrifices.

Jesus did not side with either schismatics or orthodox.
He came "to gather into one body the children of God dispersed over the whole earth." The religion He is going to
found will not be national, but universal. In the Kingdom
of God there will be no suzerain nation, no vassal nation.
The last comers, the workers of the eleventh hour, will be
treated there with the same consideration as the others.

In the temples of Christ, bulls and doves will not be
immolated. Like Melchisedech, priests will offer bread and
wine. Yet the break between the ancient worship and the
new will not be complete. Without effusion of blood,
there is no redemption. There will, therefore, be one bloody
immolation, that of Calvary, the august sacrifice of which
the Levitical holocausts were but the figure. This immolation, being of infinite value, will be accomplished once for
all. But the Christ, hidden beneath the form of the Host,
will make Himself present upon the altars in order to
renew the oblation. He will be the Pontiff of the New
Covenant, an incomparable High-Priest, or, better said, a
High-Priest that is Unique. He alone can praise the
Father, for He alone knows Him. He alone can make a

requital equal to the benefit bestowed, for He is God offering Himself to God. Thus the new worship will be worthy of the Divine Majesty.

Looking into the future, Jesus sees the churches that will spring up from the earth. Everywhere will be offered the pure oblation foretold by the prophet Malachy. As the earth rotates on its axis, presenting to the sun every part of its surface, priests are going up to the altar, so that every day the earth crowns itself with a white aureola of Hosts. A magnificent Vision, the sublime creation which was in germ in the mind and the heart of the Divine Boy.

Jesus turns His eyes towards the Well of Jacob. Thirsty from the heat and the long road He has just covered, He says to His Mother: "Give Me a drink." Mary gives Him the fresh water she has just drawn from the well. The Child drains long draughts, then turns a tender, grateful look upon her. How many times has she not quenched His thirst since that first time in the Cave of Bethlehem! She is the source of His life. But He has caused another source to spring up in her, an inexhaustible one, unto life eternal. The water of Jacob's Well slakes our thirst but for a time . . . But those that drink of the water which Jesus will give will never again thirst.

This mysterious water symbolizes supernatural life,

which gladdens us and satisfies our deepest aspirations, for it contains potentially unalloyed beatitude, without limit, without end. It is a prelude, a foretaste of Heaven.

The simple faithful will be called to this only later, when Christ's Passion will have reopened Heaven. If they believe, if they are baptized, they will be saved. But the Blessed Virgin participates in advance in all the fruits of the redemptive sacrifice. She is sanctified, predestined. Exteriorly, there is no distinction between her and the other women who come, like her, to draw water. But the eyes of Jesus, looking beneath appearances, admire the supernatural gifts with which her divine maternity has enriched her. How beautiful she is, the King's daughter! The charm of her face, the brightness of her glance are but the reflection of the loveliness of her soul.

In contradistinction to the Samaritan woman, Mary is perfectly pure, and she knows the gift of God: she knows Who it is that is speaking to her. The Archangel has revealed to her the dignity of her Son, His Mission, His future glory. He is the Son of the Most-High. As His name implies, He will save the world, and He will reign for ever over the House of Jacob, i.e. over the elect.

The Samaritan woman is a sinner, a poor unfortunate creature. Yet, despite her unworthiness, she serves Providential designs. This woman, little esteemed by her compatriots, becomes an instrument of salvation for them. She communicates to them her growing faith: "Come," she says to them, "come and see a man who has told me all things whatsoever I have done. Is not he the Christ?"

This is the rôle of Mary: to bring souls to Jesus. The town of Lourdes, a center of devotion to Mary, has become a center of devotion to the Holy Eucharist. By the favors she lavishes, by the miracles her intercession multiples, the Immaculate Virgin attracts multitudes only to lead them to her Divine Son. A pious author calls her (with an audacity that we would not dare permit ourselves) the Divine Fisherman's bait: *Esca spiritalis hami.*

The Samaritan woman was immortalized for giving Jesus a drink. Mary did the same; she was His nurse, nurse of the natural Christ, and of the mystical Christ. Every grace comes to us through her, not only in the sense that she gave birth to Our Saviour, but in the sense that all divine favors pass through her hands. She is God's Almoner, the treasurer of Paradise. In the economy of the Redemption, she, therefore, holds a considerable place. The world was lost by one woman; it is by the New Eve that it is saved.

These thoughts, crowding upon Jesus' mind, arouse in Him a lively enthusiasm. Around Jacob's Well, as far as the eye can see, stretch fields of waving wheat. The rains and heat of spring have made it grow fast; in a few weeks it will be ready to reap. How magnificent a harvest will be that of souls! How fine the generation that will throng the courts of the New Jerusalem! One world is ending: another world is beginning. The first Adam begot a sinful, corrupt, wretched humanity. The second Adam will give birth to a people of saints. To those who believe in Him, He will give power to become the children of God.

And Jesus recalls the prophetic vision of Isaias: "Arise, Jerusalem, for thy light is come, . . . For behold darkness shall cover the earth, and a mist the people: but the Lord shall arise upon thee and his glory shall be seen upon thee. . . . Lift up thy eyes round about, and see, . . . and thy heart shall wonder and be enlarged, . . . thy sons shall come from afar, . . . all they from Saba shall come, bringing gold and frankincense, and showing forth praise to the Lord." But a shadow passes over His face. If the harvest is abundant, the reapers are few. The Father of the family calls repeatedly, but many have not the courage to renounce all things to follow Him. They are willing enough to be served by religion, they are not eager to serve it. And how many others, after putting their hand to the plough, look back and return to the goods they had quitted!

What saddens the Divine Boy also is the prevision of His partial failure. Human liberty will checkmate Him. Numbers will close their ears to His word, will refuse to believe it, and even curse Him Who comes to save them. For them Christ's blood will be shed in vain: their sin will be even greater than if salvation had not been offered them.

O mystery of the blindness of men, almost as incomprehensible as the Redemption itself!

To-day, Jesus is again thinking thoughts like these. From His Tabernacle He follows our goings and comings. He awaits a visit, or at least an act of faith and love. He asks nothing but to do us good; He thirsts to give Himself; *sitit sitiri,* He thirsts to be thirsted for, He wants to be wanted. But alas! how many pass His churches, indifferent, heedless, perhaps even contemptuous! They are plagued by passions, crushed under the burden of life, discouraged, bitter, desperate. Jesus offers them the drink that refreshes, strengthens, renders immortal, . . . and they turn their eyes away.

Contemporary society is like a meadow dried up by a

scorching wind, the grass is burned, the flowers with-
ered. Down yonder gushes an inexhaustible spring, with
water enough to revive the whole vast plain. But around
it men have built a wall: a high, thick wall of indifference, unbelief, hatred. They would rather perish than
hold out a hand to God.

Ah! if Jesus were not impassible, how He would suffer
at such a sight! How His Sacred Heart would bleed once
more!

Merciful Saviour, have pity on the souls that are being
lost. Dispel the prejudices that estrange them from You.
Raise up legions of apostles with hearts aflame with zeal
to pull the unbelieving masses from the mire in which
they are wallowing, and lift them to the heights where
You reign. You came to give us supernatural life; since
men have rejected this divine gift, their natural life lan-
guishes and breaks down. Those who no longer believe
in Heaven make this world a Hell. O Love, come to the
aid of this miserable society, dying because it does not
love You!

XVI

JESUS IN THE TEMPLE

IT WAS at the Feast of the Pasch that Jesus went to the Temple for the first time. With His parents He celebrated the legal Supper, according to the rites established by Moses even to the most trifling detail. A lamb that had been offered in the Temple was roasted; it had to be completely consumed at one meal, which leads us to believe that the Holy Family must have joined other relatives of the house of Anna and Joachim.

The guests stood around the table, girt as if on the point of departing on a journey. This attitude recalled the precipitate flight of the Hebrews, escaping from the yoke of Pharaoh. The legal Pasch commemorated the crossing of the Red Sea and the march to the Promised Land.

But on the eve of His death, Jesus was to institute another Pasch, whose significance is incomparably deeper and more beautiful. The Christian Feast symbolizes the passing from earth to Heaven by the way that Christ opened for us at so great a cost! *Pascha nostrum immolatus est Christus*. He was to be immolated for the salvation of the world. When He celebrated the Pasch at Jerusalem, the Divine Boy was not ignorant of this; and in the lamb, served whole, with its forelegs extended on skewers forming a cross, He saw a striking image of His own crucifixion.

According to the Law of Moses, care had to be taken in carving the ritual lamb, not to break a bone of him. Thus Christ's members were not broken on the Cross as were the thieves! But to ensure His death, one of the soldiers pierced His side with a lance.

This Passion, so desired by Jesus as Saviour, He dreaded as man. Yet His face betrayed no emotion. He maintained His habitual gentle serenity. Among the relatives who surrounded Him, not one suspected the bloody Cross that rose on the horizon for Him.

When the Galilean caravan, of which the Holy Family formed part, took the homeward road, Jesus did not follow it. Jerusalem, the city where He was to die, had fascinated Him. He passed His days in the Temple, following the lessons of the Doctors expounding the text of the Bible. Sometimes He would put questions to them with deference; and all marveled at His extraordinary and precocious intelligence. Their surprise, says the Gospel, rose to stupefaction: *Stupebant omnes.* A ray of the light that He so carefully hid, was filtering out as it were, and allowing them to surmise in Him a storehouse of wonders.

In spite of the sympathetic atmosphere that surrounded Him, Jesus could not forget the Passion which the Paschal Lamb had so vividly recalled and depicted before His eyes. Amongst these Doctors in Israel, looking at Him with an admiring and affectionate smile, several will one day be His judges. When Caiaphas asks them: "What think you?" they will answer with one voice: "He is guilty of death!" Forgetful of their dignity, these members of the Sanhedrim will climb the hill of Calvary to insult His agony. They will hiss and shake their fists at Him, saying: "Vah! thou that didst call thyself the Son of God, come down from the cross!"

To-day they see in Jesus only a handsome boy whose future promises to be glorious. They admire Him, as we admire the rosebud or the sprouting wheat. Jesus will be teaching in Solomon's Porch, and holding His audience spellbound by the charm of His words . . . in the not far distant future. He will perform miracles, crowds will run after Him, and His growing popularity will alarm these men in high places. Still more disquieting to them will be His doctrine. If it should prevail, farewell to the privileges of the Temple, to the tribe of Levi, to the Jewish nation! Thus self-interest, jealousy, national pride, all the passions (under the cloak of zeal, and therefore all the more violent) will conspire against Christ. He will be an imposter, a disturber of the peace, a dangerous innovator, . . . He must die for the safety of the people!

How many Christians, alas! resemble these Doctors of the Law! When things go well with them, when **God** grants them the temporal favors they desire, they recognize that piety is useful for all sorts of things, that it holds promises for the future life and for the present also; and full of gratitude they cry out: "Hosanna to the Son of David!" But when God tries them by sickness, by poverty, by the death of dear ones; what recriminations! they rebel, they blaspheme; and like the Jews, insane with rage, they are tempted to mutter: "Away with Him! Crucify Him!" If they do not pronounce these words, they *act* them at least, for, according to the Epistle to the Hebrews, those who violate the Law of God in grave matter, deliberately, crucify again Christ Jesus.

Before casting a stone at these poor sinners, let us take a look at ourselves. At bottom, has not each one of us an Anti-Christ? It is our "old man," everything in our nature which "kicks against the goad" of the Gospel. This carnal man we long ago condemned to death, but did we really execute him? Which of us would dare to say of ourselves those words of St. Thérèse of Lisieux:

"Since I was three years old, I have never refused God anything"?

When Mary finds her Son again in the Temple, joy floods her heart, joy enhanced by the admiration she reads on the faces of the Doctors. The growing glory of Jesus is reflected upon His parents.

He left them, it is true, without warning, and threw them into consternation and distress. But they know the secret of His birth; the Son of the Most-High is not subject to the common law. Thus with admirable delicacy, Mary confines herself to her anguish. She knows how to reconcile the respect she owes to her Divine Son and her maternal authority. Her reproach is tender: "Son, why hast Thou done so to us? Behold, Thy father and I have sought Thee sorrowing." And He said to them: "How is it that you sought Me? Did you not know that I must be about My Father's business?" A mysterious answer, of which Mary and Joseph did not grasp all the implications. Some commentators interpret it thus: "Why did you seek Me elsewhere than in the Temple? If you had known Me, you would have come straight here, and you would have spared yourselves much anxiety."

Such is not, in our opinion, the sense of the divine words. Jesus means: You should not have been anxious.

I came into the world to do the Will of My Father in Heaven. If I left you for awhile, it was to do His work. Knowing My origin, you should have trusted Me, and left Me full freedom of action. Later, when I shall be obliged to separate from you, to expose Myself to the attacks of My enemies and finally to climb the hill of Calvary, do not be distressed, but submit, like Me, to the Heavenly Father's Will.

Christian children are sometimes forced to speak to their parents in a similar way; for instance, when their vocation is opposed. The case is not infrequent. Some imagine that their child is lost to them when he gives himself to God. If a daughter marries a Colonial official, they willingly consent to her expatriating herself for ten or even twenty years, because she is still of the family. But if she consecrates herself to the apostolate, to the service of the poor or the sick, she is a stranger whom they renounce. It is an absurd prejudice, for in religious life affections are not destroyed; far from it, lifted to a supernatural plane, they are at once purer and livelier.

Thus, when the chosen one has done all he can to convince his family, and can no longer defer action without danger to his vocation, he must have the courage to say: "My dear parents, if my country were attacked and called me to the colors, and you were trying to prevent me from doing my duty, I should have to say to you: 'I belong first to my country, then to you.' It is God Who is calling me now, your Master and mine. Before belonging to you, I belong to Him. Let me go then, and you will be doing God's Will as I am doing it myself."

"I must be about My Father's business." How beautiful and how fruitful our life would be if this maxim inspired our every act! God made all things for Himself, that He might be known, loved and served. Our life is given us, therefore, not for the purpose of our sanctification and salvation, as many imagine, but for the glory of God. To this supreme end everything else must be subordinated. A great patriot exclaimed one day:

France, will'st thou my blood, It is all thine, my France!
   Need'st thou my suffering?
   Pain shall be Law for me;
Need'st thou my death? Then welcome, Death! . . . for
   thee!
   But live thou on, my France! [1]

The religious sentiment must be more ardent than patriotism for its object is more excellent. If our destruction could serve the designs of God, we should be glad to be blotted out. But let us hasten to add that such is not the

[1] Paul Déroulède, *Songs of the Soldier.*

case. God, Who is Wisdom itself, harmonizes all things; His interests and ours, His own glory and our beatitude. We achieve perfection and attain to bliss in proportion to our fidelity in His service. Confiding in His goodness, let us keep our inward eye fixed upon Him, let us live for Him alone. Let us "seek first the Kingdom of God and His justice, and all things shall be added unto us."

XVII

"Whatsoever He Shall Say to You, Do Ye"

At the marriage feast of Cana, Mary appears; she acts, she speaks. In the Gospel narrative, so brief but so rich in meaning, we see one trait of her character very clearly delineated, . . . the most exquisite delicacy. It is also on this occasion that she inaugurates the function which she still continues to exercise, i.e. that of Mediatrix.

Seeing the embarrassment of the young couple when the wine gave out (they were, perhaps, poor), Mary turns to her divine Son, and whispers simply: "They have no wine."

In her discreet reserve, she does not insist. She does not beseech Jesus to work a miracle. She merely calls His attention to the need of the guests and the confusion of the host and hostess: it was a delicate way of appealing to the compassion and the power of her Son. There is a picture that represents her holding in her hand an empty cup upside down; a rather vulgar gesture, which Mary certainly never made.

Jesus replies, also in a low voice: "What is that to me and to thee?" an expression equivalent to "Why do you worry?" and He continues: "My hour is not yet come." If He makes use of this (to us) rather enigmatic expression, it is because Mary understood it. She was His confidant during the long years of His hidden life. He had doubtless told her that when His hour should come He would preach the Gospel and work miracles. But the hour fixed by the eternal decree was not yet.

Mary's indirect request seems refused. But the maternal heart has quick intuitions. By His smile and the tone of His voice, she understands that her prayer is granted, in spite of appearances, and turning to the waiters, she says: "Whatsoever He shall say to you, do ye." *p. 129*

We are not surprised to find this exquisite delicacy in Jesus also: like mother, like Son. He has the art of teaching or correcting without wounding, of satisfying one of our desires without running counter to others.

When He began His public life, He did not proclaim: "I am the Messias, the Son of God." Who would have believed Him? There was so obvious a discrepancy between the carpenter of Nazareth, poor, obscure, without credit or prestige, and the triumphant conqueror expected by the carnal Jews! The premature revelation of the dogmas of the Trinity and the Incarnation would have shocked or angered the adorers of One God, unique, pure Spirit. Therefore, with what tact, what discreet precaution, He prepares His compatriots to receive the light: He brings the dawn before the sun. He lives a holy life, multiplies miracles, in a word, performs divine works, and lets the truth become gradually clear in souls of faith.

After the Resurrection, when He joined the disciples going to Emmaus, He did not say: "I am the Jesus of Whom you are talking." But He explains clearly and warmly the Scripture texts concerning the Messias; and He renews the ceremony of the Last Supper. And then their eyes are opened; they recognize Him in the last proof of love that He gave us: the breaking of Bread.

Jesus predicted to the Jews imminent calamities. Because they had rejected the One sent by God, their city should be destroyed, their nation cast off, their privileges abolished. But He does not announce bluntly these hard and humiliating truths. He insinuates rather than proclaims them. He tempers and softens them by veiling them in parables.

But this delicacy of the divine Heart is shown nowhere better than when He remonstrates with St. Peter. After the second miraculous draught of fishes, He takes Peter aside, so as not to humble him before the others. Is He going to overwhelm him with reproaches? to say to him, for instance, "Thou art no longer the Rock, the Cornerstone, upon which I wished to found My Church; Thou hast betrayed My confidence and scandalized thy brethren." No, He asks him gently: "Simon, son of John, lovest thou me?"

It was a natural question; after having been forsaken, denied, had not Jesus the right to be dubious about the affection of His Apostle? He does not call him Peter, but Simon, to imply that he has fallen from his high estate, that he no longer deserves to govern the Church. He says it, or rather, He implies it, He lets it be understood,—but how delicately!

Three times He puts the question. Peter is astonished by this insistence, he grows sad. Then it flashes upon him that by this triple protestation of love, Jesus is making him repair his threefold denial. Then, with a spontaneous eagerness, a sincerity that must have gone to the Master's Heart, he exclaims: "Lord, Thou knowest all things, Thou knowest that I love Thee." Thou seest the bottom of my heart.

"Feed My lambs, feed My sheep," answers Jesus, as though to say: "Since the sin is confessed, regretted, repaired, I give thee back My confidence. Thou art and thou shalt remain the head of My Church."

Truly it would be hard to imagine a more gracious vengeance; and one understands the irresistible attraction that Jesus exercised over all who followed Him. How could one fail to become attached to Him as soon as one began to know Him? How could one fail to admire the treasures of His rich nature, and particularly the marvelous art He had to touch and to win hearts?

It is probable that the young couple at Cana had not asked Mary to intervene in their behalf; but the shame and dismay on their faces must have been a silent supplication. Have we not often seen the poor, standing silent at a door, not even stretching out a hand, just looking their appeal, while their rags and infirmities plead for them? So at times the soul is satisfied to display its wretchedness before the eyes of Him Who sees all things. "My God," exclaimed Ernest Hello one day, "I am like a dried-up torrent, that remembering the coolness and the abundance of its waters, by its silence invokes the rain!"

When our request is explicit, we are fond of placing it in Mary's hands. Is she not our official advocate, since she is our mother? It is especially the grace of forgiveness that we implore through her intercession. We feel that in spite of her purity, or rather, because of its perfection in her, she is full of indulgence for us. A pious author calls our attention to the fact that between Jesus and the Penitent Thief on Calvary, stood Mary at the foot of her Son's Cross.

Mary is our Mediatrix also in this sense, that by her beauty, by her kindness, by the charm that emanates from her whole personality, she draws souls to God. She is like the bait that God makes use of to catch souls.

At Cana, just as in our own day, Mary leads souls to Jesus. She urges us to believe in Him, to follow His directions: "Whatsoever He shall tell you, do it" . . . simple words, but how full in their simplicity!

Do.—True piety is not merely the observance of certain rites or the repetition of certain formulas. Neither does it consist in tender feelings that express themselves in sighs and tears. This sensible fervor is good and desirable, but not essential. The true friends of God can be recognized by this sign, that they have no will but His. *Idem velle, idem nolle, id demum amicitia est,* one of the ancients used to say. And Jesus Himself says to us: "You are My friends if you keep My commandments." If, in order to please Him, it sufficed to recite the Act of Love every day, it would really be too easy. Jesus wants us to love Him as He Himself has loved us. Now He was not satisfied to say from the height of Heaven: "I am sorry for you," leaving us in our misery. No, He came down upon the earth, He became an Infant, He died on the Cross. True love pre-supposes, therefore, self-renunciation and the spirit of sacrifice. Those who love God otherwise than in words brave inconveniences to observe His Law and to avoid sin which offends Him.

Do Whatsoever He Will Say to You.—God makes known His Will by His commandments, His precepts, by the orders of legitimate superiors and by events. When misfortune threatens us, we may, indeed we should, do all in our power to avert it. But if our efforts are vain, what is to be done? Repine, blaspheme, as many bad Christians do? No, but bow our head beneath the Hand that strikes and say: "My God, not my will but Thine be done."

God speaks to us also by the voice of our conscience. He inspires us with sorrow for our sins and the desire to lead a better life. He is the soul of our soul. Not a day, not an hour passes that He does not intervene in our spiritual life. He is the conscience of our conscience. But to hear Him, we must lend an attentive ear. His voice is like the sound of distant music. He respects the free-will He has bestowed upon us, and does not impose His own. Before opening our door, He knocks. If He is denied entrance, He withdraws. But when He is eagerly welcomed, He enters, and the mystery of divine intimacy begins in the recollected soul.

Do *whatsoever,* i.e. *all, everything,* He tells you:—No one can flatter himself that He fulfills the Law, if he violates a single article of it. No one can assert that he loves God if, on one single point, he neglects or omits to conform to His Will. How many Christians, alas! are in this situation! When their conscience demands certain sacrifices, they reply: "I am quite ready to make this one, but not *that!*" "*That*" is precisely the one that God holds to most, and as long as one resists Him there is no progress. One would like to launch out into the deep and casts off some moorings, but one cable holds, and, because of it, our vessel remains stationary, if not pulling back.

The Gospel abounds in simple statements that open vast perspectives to the inward eye. Mary's words belong in this category. It sums up the whole Christian asceticism. To attain perfection one single condition is necessary and sufficient: to listen to God's voice and to obey immediately. Nothing is simpler, nothing more difficult.

It supposes a vigilance of every instant, a total abnegation, a persevering effort, sustained by ardent love.

O Virgin Mary, You who show us the way to Heaven, obtain for us the courage to persevere in it to the end. May we, following Your counsel and example, keep our eyes fixed upon Your Divine Son and do whatsoever He will say to us!

XVIII

The Ninth Beatitude

Let us recall the exordium of the Sermon on the Mount:

"Blessed are the poor in spirit: for theirs is the Kingdom of Heaven. Blessed are the meek: for they shall possess the land. Blessed are they that mourn: for they shall be comforted. Blessed are they that hunger and thirst after justice: for they shall have their fill. Blessed are the merciful: for they shall obtain mercy. Blessed are the clean of heart: for they shall see God. Blessed are the peacemakers: for they shall be called the children of God. Blessed are they that suffer persecution for justice sake: for theirs is the Kingdom of Heaven." (Matt. V:3-10)

Of whom was Jesus thinking as He drew this portrait of the ideal Christian? What model presented itself to His inward eye? Himself, assuredly, and perhaps also His Mother. Mary was His first disciple. No one was more penetrated with His spirit; no one understood it better or practised its teachings more perfectly. Each

The Mother of Jesus

Beatitude, therefore, presents us an aspect of Mary's character.

Like her divine Son, she was detached from everything; in the poor dwelling at Nazareth, she divided her time between prayer and manual work. She was at peace, —with God, . . . with herself, . . . with everyone. Nothing equaled her purity, her meekness, her compassion for all unfortunates. She hungered and thirsted for justice, not for herself, the most perfect of women, but for others. With what ardor the Queen of the Apostles recited the prayer taught by the Divine Master: "Our Father, . . . hallowed be Thy Name, Thy Kingdom come!" She often wept. She was persecuted in the person of Jesus: she suffered every outrage inflicted upon Him; on Calvary, she was crucified with Him, and that is why "all generations shall call her *blessed!*"

One day when Jesus was preaching with His usual eloquence, a woman exclaimed in her enthusiasm: "Blessed is the womb that bore Thee!" And Jesus replied: "Yea, rather, blessed are they that hear the word of God and keep it!" (Luke, XI:27-28)

This is what might be called the Ninth Beatitude. When formulating it, Jesus seems to divert attention from His Mother, and to some His words sound harsh. Although in the intimacy of home-life, they say,

134

He was full of deference for His parents, in public He kept them in the background, He ignored them, fearing that He might be suspected of being influenced by them. He required His disciples to quit home and family; ought He not set them the example Himself?

Another episode in the Gospel is cited in connection with this. One day, Jesus was teaching in a house, when some one came to Him and said: "Thy Mother and Thy brethren are without, desiring to see Thee." He replied: "Who is My Mother and who are My brethren?" And fixing His eyes on His disciples, He added: "My Mother and My brethren are they who hear the word of God and do it." (Luke, VIII:19-22)

But who can fail to perceive that these words which seem meant to disparage Mary and relegate her to the background, really extol her and place her in the forefront? If beatitude consists in hearkening to God's commands and obeying them to the letter, never was any creature more blessed than Mary. Never did she hesitate to do her duty, never did she shrink or recoil before a sacrifice.

In this respect, as in so many others, she is amazingly like Jesus. The *Fiat* of the Annunciation recalls the *Fiat* of Gethsemane, and we know the influence of these two assents upon the destinies of the world, the destinies of the human race. If Jesus, yielding to fear, had refused to drink the bitter chalice, the redemptive plan would have been modified. The like would have happened if Mary, terrified at the honor proposed to her by God, with the trials inseparable from any great destiny, had not given her consent. But she accepted her glory and the price she would have to pay for it; Jesus accepted the direst humiliations and the most cruel death, and the world was saved.

Later, Mary had to pronounce another *Fiat* still more meritorious. Jesus, Who had announced His approaching Passion to His disciples, made it His duty to prepare His Mother for it. A Mystery-Play of the Middle Ages supposes that on the eve of the great immolation, Mary endeavored to dissuade her Son, if not from giving Himself up to His enemies, at least from enduring such excruciating pain. Is not one single drop of His blood sufficient to save the world?

With medieval simplicity the quaint dialogue proceeds:

Mary.

My Son, be pleased, of Thy kind grace,
To die a quick and painless death!

Jesus.

Mother, in bitterness and pain
Thy Son must draw His latest breath.

136

Mary.

Upon the earth, and without moan!

Jesus.

Upon a Cross Thy Son must groan!

Mary.

Let not Thy precious Blood be shed!

Jesus.

The very earth with Blood is red!
I shall be stretched and pulled about,
Till men My ev'ry bone may count . . .
Then shall they pierce My Hands and Feet,
Nor deem e'en then their work complete.

Mary.

Harsh answers these Thou givest me,
Thy mother, Son, that bore Thee!

Jesus.

The Scriptures must accomplished be!
My Father's Will's before Me!

Pathetic as the scene is, even medieval naïveté must
have felt it improbable! The valiant woman who stood
beneath the Cross, would have exhorted her Son to do
the Father's Will to the very end. The next day, when

she beheld this new Isaac climbing the hill of Calvary, tottering under the crushing weight of His gibbet, she encouraged Him by her look: "Go on, my Son. Obey, even unto death, and the death of the Cross; it is for the glory of God and the salvation of the world."

One can picture a mother to whom a tenderly loved son confides his vocation. He is to be a missionary; he is going to leave for a distant country, whence, doubtless, he will never return. It is a cruel separation; but in such circumstances a valiant Christian suppresses her natural feelings. "Lord," she says, "before he was mine, my son was Yours. I shall not try to hold him back, Thy Will be done, not mine."

Still more painful was the sacrifice asked of Mary. She had to consent to her Son's Passion; a soul that loves, resigns herself more easily to her own sufferings than to those of the loved one. Nevertheless, she acquiesced generously in the Divine Will. She offered as a victim the flesh of her flesh. Below the Fourth Station of the Way of the Cross, one would like to read this inscription: *Vult mortem ejus quem amat Salvatoris mater.* "The Saviour's mother wills the death of Him she loves."

Father Faber (in Chapter VII of *At the Foot of the Cross*) reckons that a saint corresponds perhaps to the thousandth part of the graces he receives. Upon what does he base his calculations? I do not know. But if he is correct, he gives us a high idea of Mary's perfection. We call her the Queen of All Saints because she excels them all, not only by her dignity as Mother of God, but because of the splendor of her sanctity. Never did she say "No" to God; and this was why her spiritual life was a continuous enrichment. One grace attracts another. When we are collaborating with God, when we put no obstacle in His way, He carries out His plan. He makes each one of us a sanctuary where He loves to dwell. Mary was the most beautiful of these spiritual Temples: a Tower of Ivory, a House of Gold, perfect in matter and form.

Our great misfortune is that we do not allow God to finish His work in us. The foundations of the work have been laid by heredity, by our first education. The day comes when God asks us to contribute to our formation and to work with Him. But, alas! many refuse to cooperate, some even oppose His action. They do not always resist the seduction to evil, and at last sin, like a devastating hurricane that uproots and demolishes, wrecks the edifice, leaving it like a rough attempt at building, or a ruin. Hence the sadness, spoken of by Léon Bloy, the sadness at not being saints. Mary never knew that sadness. She was what she was meant to be, and the consciousness of her perfection flooded her humble soul with a deep and penetrating joy.

The accomplishment of the Divine Will is then the secret of perfection and of happiness. Events that upset our plans are the principal cause of our griefs. But are not these events willed or permitted by God? Yes, of course, and we believe it; but what hinders our mind from perceiving this truth is that we look at it from a narrow angle, namely, our own personal interest, or that of our family, our firm, our country. What do we generally want but success, a comfortable life, temporal prosperity? We forget that our planet is a tiny portion of the universe. God takes care of it as well as of the thousands of suns scattered through limitless space. He created them for His glory, i.e. that He might be known, loved, and served by His rational creatures. To accomplish His designs, He uses means which at times disconcert us. Why epidemics, volcanic eruptions, wars, persecutions? But let us have faith in His Wisdom which infinitely surpasses ours, and we shall find peace. If our love were more living, even the little we have for God would extend to the events willed or permitted by Him. All that comes from Him is good. Our life would be one *Amen,* or one continual *Alleluia!* Like St. John Chrysostom when he was dying, we should be repeating constantly: "In all things let us give thanks to God."

And this peace which it is possible for us to enjoy here below is but the prelude to supreme felicity. "In Heaven," says St. John, "we shall be like to Him, for we shall see Him as He is."

XIX

BLESSED IS THE WOMB THAT
BORE THEE!

WHEN the time came to preach the Gospel, Jesus had to leave His Mother. Doubtless the separation was neither complete nor final. In the course of His continual peregrinations the divine Preacher returned to Nazareth from time to time; and Mary joined Him more than once at Capharnaum, at Jerusalem and elsewhere. But it was the end of the sweet intimacy of family life.

And what shall we say of Mary's anxieties when she thought of the perils that surrounded Jesus! He had powerful enemies: the Pharisees, the priestly caste, the princes to whom His popularity gave umbrage! What was to be the end of this movement He was promoting? At the beginning of His public life, Mary did not know; but she could not forget Simeon's prophecy, and at times anguish engulfed her soul.

In spite of it all, she was happy, so happy as to make her companions jealous. Witness the woman who cried out one day from the midst of the crowd: "Blessed is the womb that bore Thee!" If Mary was also present, she must have thrilled with justifiable gladness. Yes, the Almighty had favored her, she was blessed amongst women.

Imagine a mother whose only son, unusually gifted, has rapidly attained the highest honors. His rise has not dazzled him. Far from denying his parentage, he is full of consideration and attentions for his family, and shares with them all his wealth.

What for most mothers is but a dream, for Mary was a reality. Jesus of Nazareth rose in a few months from obscurity to fame. By His eloquence, by His goodness, by His miracles, He excited the enthusiasm of the crowds that followed Him, crying: "A great prophet hath arisen in our midst, and God hath visited His people!"

This swift ascension did not surprise Mary. At Nazareth she had watched Him growing up, displaying gradually the spiritual treasures that He concealed within. And now this divine flower, that had remained so long in the shade, was blossoming out in full sunshine. It was attracting all eyes, it was becoming more and more beautiful, so that each day as it came was looked forward to in expectation of a new revelation.

Mary delighted in this beauty, and all the more as it was partly her work. In one sense, Jesus had formed

His Mother. In fact, it was with a view to the Incarnation that she had been decked with every virtue, dowered with every grace. When He fashioned her body and soul, God conformed to the law of heredity that He Himself had established. He endowed her with the qualities which (humanly speaking) she was to transmit to her Divine Son. She was therefore the Dawn of the Sun of Justice; she was the "Christ Begun."

Later, Jesus completed her formation. He announced to her the approaching Kingdom of God; He taught her the admirable doctrine that was to regenerate the world, and none ever listened to His words with a more attentive ear.

But, as we read in the Epistle to the Hebrews, Christ wished to resemble His brethren in all things. In His development, He followed the common law. He did not form Himself alone. It was Mary who taught Him to walk, to talk, to say vocal prayers. His Mother's lessons were, if not the cause, at least the occasion of His progress. To all appearances, all happened as if Mary had really been the educatrix of Jesus.

When Jesus was preaching so eloquently to the listening throngs, when He was passing through the country doing good, she had the right to be proud of Him. She took part in His success, she rejoiced in His triumphs, not only because she was identified with Him by love, but because she had contributed to His formation.

It happens to us also to do good through others and to rejoice in their success.

When a child is born into the world, its parents may say: "Life has not been propitious to us. It has not fulfilled our hopes and expectations; but our child shall be better and happier than we!"

The child that evokes such hopes is welcome. He has the beauty of the dawn that heralds a radiant day, the beauty of the blossom that promises the luscious fruit, the beauty of the sprouting wheat that forecasts a rich harvest. Beside his cradle all hopes are permissible.

This is the hope that sustains the parents through all the difficulties of their arduous task. What expense, what weariness, what anxieties it involves! But also what a magnificent reward they sometimes reap! When they have turned out a man of real worth, they rise with him to eminence and take a glorious revenge on life!

When the harvest has failed, the farmer does not become discouraged. He ploughs the field and sows again, looking to the future hopefully. It is the same with the human race. It works in hopes that the coming generations will attain the ideal vainly pursued hitherto. "Better than we, to-morrow's men shall be!"

The Mother of Jesus

Always disappointed, it is always just as credulous. This mad race towards the Promised Land, this obstinate straining towards a goal that eludes the hand just about to grasp it, . . . is there anything more heroic and more heart-breaking!

In like manner it is the hope of surviving oneself and even of being "self-surpassed" that sustains the educator. If it is not in his power to achieve success, he wants at least to deserve it. Frustrated in one attempt, he sets to work again. What delight when he succeeds in forming good citizens, devoted to the public weal rather than to self-interest; or again, men of high principle, Christians of convictions, militant Christians! Sure that they will carry on his work, he calls to them confidently in the words of one of our poets:

> Content thee not with being good, my son;—Be thou divine!
> Go forth, and nobly spend thyself, not counting!— Speak and act!
> Let thine eye's broadened sweep at once embrace All space, all time,—to nothing human strange!
> Make of thy heart, fond and insatiable A deep abyss of love, . . . that God may fill! [1]

[1] R. Valéry-Radot.

It has been said that under the "Ancien Régime," the people (meaning the working classes) admired the luxury of the Court. Themselves in meagre circumstances, and often in want, they liked to see their King rich and happy for all.

That these sentiments can have been very common, we are at liberty to doubt. But it is quite certain that the fervent Christian regards as his own the glory of the Christ he loves. It is with all his heart that he sings the liturgical prayer: *Gratias agimus tibi propter magnam gloriam tuam.* "We give Thee thanks for Thy great glory." The immense glory of Christ is a good common to Him and to all those who form part of His Mystical Body.

Bossuet wrote in this sense to one of his correspondents: "Rejoice with Jesus Christ that He is the most beautiful of the sons of man; and remember that we must count amongst His beauties the goodness He has shown in wishing to win our hearts to fill them with Himself."

A religious who was critically ill was asked how he felt: "Very ill," he replied, "but God is well; that's enough!"

The contemplatives loved to meditate long hours upon the attributes of God: His holiness, His immensity, His

goodness, and especially His beatitude. This is according to the words of the Gospel, to "enter into the joy
of their Lord." This divine joy is like a bottomless and
shoreless ocean into which they plunge with transport.

The destitute who heard from afar sounds of the revel-
ries, the festivities of the Court of Versailles knew well
enough that they would never take part in them. Such
amusements, such splendors were not for them. But
divine happiness is not a thing foreign to us. We are
not merely God's subjects, but His adoptive children.
Baptism has made us the brothers of Christ, and consequently, co-heirs with Him. If we are faithful to our
vocation, if our conduct is in conformity with our dignity, we shall live eternally as God does, and with the
same life. The sanctifying grace which we possess is like
a seed which grows and develops here below and will
one day blossom in glory.

May this prospect strengthen us and make us forget
the troubles of the present. The world is growing more
and more materialistic: it sets no store upon the spiritual
values deposited in Christianity. We are storm-tossed
mariners, but a light-house in the distance shows us the
house of our Heavenly Father. There is a place there
prepared for us: let us not lose it by our own fault!

XX

THE VIRGIN OF THE GRAPES

IN AN old Chapel in Brittany, they venerate a picture of the Blessed Virgin with her Divine Child on her lap. Her right arm is around Him, with her left hand she offers Him a bunch of grapes. Is it not a delicate allusion to the Holy Eucharist? This Child Whom she is bringing up with such tender solicitude is one day to be a Victim for us; countless faithful souls will be fed with bread changed into His Body and wine that has become His Blood.

Jesus, Who had announced His approaching Passion to His disciples, did not fail to prepare His Mother for what was before her. It was for Him a duty of gratitude and filial piety. "Do not be distressed," He doubtless said to her, "I shall not leave thee lonely. Hidden in the Host, I shall live near thee, with thee, in thee. It is expedient for thee that I go, for after My visible form has disappeared, our intimacy will be greater than during the years of My Public Life, when we were so often separated."

When Fra Angelico painted the Last Supper, he rep-

149

resented the Blessed Virgin kneeling beside the table where the Apostles were receiving their First Communion. Was this simply an artistic fancy? Let us not think so. If Mary did not actually assist at the institution of the Holy Eucharist, she was present in spirit. She knew what Jesus meant to do at the Last Supper: to substitute for the legal Pasch a new sacrifice, which would extend to all times and to all countries the benefits of the Incarnation.

To obey the Master's injunction: "Do this in commemoration of Me," the first Christians frequently celebrated the Supper of the Lord. At the end of a repast taken in common, a priest recited the Lord's Prayer; then he took bread, said "This is My Body" and divided the consecrated bread among the guests. He blessed and consecrated in like manner a cup of wine, which was passed from one to another around the table. It seemed to them like seeing Christ Himself, once more amidst His disciples, renewing the touching ceremony of Holy Thursday.

With what disposition did Mary take part in this agape? The same, evidently, as during that mysterious Communion of nine months, from the day of the Annunciation until the day of His Nativity.

FAITH.—The Archangel Gabriel had announced to her that she was to become a mother by the operation of the Holy Ghost. And now another mystery, no less disconcerting to human reason is proposed to her: the Incarnate Word really present under the appearance of the Host. Yet this mystery is not more difficult to believe than the other. Nothing is impossible to God. Divine love tends to perfect union, and as it is served by infinite Wisdom and Power, it is not to be checked or thwarted by any obstacle.

Like John, her adopted son, Mary believed in God's love for us. When, therefore, she had received the consecrated Bread, with what faith she must have looked upon it! Her eyes of flesh saw in it but the appearance of bread, but her inward eye, more enlightened, saw deeper and discerned the Son of God. She adored Him under the form of Bread as she had formerly adored Him under the form of a frail, crying Babe.

PURITY.—The Ark of the Covenant was made of precious cedar-wood overlaid with gold. Yet it contained nothing but the Tables of the Law and a pot of Manna. How much richer and purer should be the first Tabernacle of the New Law! God made a spotless one to receive, as R. P. Henrion says: "the living and essential Purity." Immaculate in her conception, Mary was Immaculate in her life as well; never did she commit the slightest fault; never was she tempted, in the strict sense of the word. In this virginal soul where nothing offends His eye, Jesus in the Host dwelt with pleasure. Since then, the world has never seen a spiritual Temple comparable to His first abode.

HUMILITY.—If Mary had been less humble she might have said to herself: "If I have been chosen to be the mother of the Saviour, it was because of my eminent sanctity." But never did such a thought enter her mind. She thought, on the contrary, that it was by a wholly gratuitous favor that she had been called to so high a destiny. The Almighty had selected her, but merely to carry out His designs; He could have made use of another instrument.

With the same humility Mary took part in the Holy Mysteries. "What am I, O my God," she said, "that Thou shouldst deign to visit me? I am not worthy to receive Thee." All the saints have thus prostrated themselves before God. Pride and corruption go together frequently, but the purer a soul is, the humbler it becomes.

CHARITY.—All mothers love the child they are about to bring into the world. But they love it without knowing it; it is but an ideal which they fashion and adorn to suit their taste. It was not so in Mary's case. She was bearing a priceless treasure. How she loved Him, therefore! . . . with all her heart, with all her strength, with all the ardor God Himself asks of our love! Her piety was mingled with her maternal tenderness, since her Child was also her God; and these two feelings, taking color each from the other, reinforcing each other, form a whole of unutterable sweetness. Mary's life, while she was bearing beneath her heart the Incarnate Word, was one continual ecstasy.

Now she lived over again in her Communions those delicious hours. She became once again the Ark of the Covenant, since the Author of the Gospel Law resided within her, the Living Bread that giveth life to the world. What must have been the fervor of her thanksgivings! What the charm of those conversations with her Jesus living once more within her! It would need the purity of an angel to penetrate these mysteries!

DESIRE.—And yet Mary's happiness was not complete; an impenetrable veil separated her from her Beloved. During the weeks which preceded the Nativity she longed to contemplate the face of the Child Whose presence she felt. At each Communion she must have felt a similar longing. She possessed Jesus without seeing Him. Something was lacking to her joy. She felt it keenly, and knowing that death alone could satisfy her desire, she said with St. Paul: "I desire to be dissolved and to be with Jesus!" Oh! to go there above, where Christ is sitting at the right hand of the Father, to find Him again with no more fear of losing Him, to live happy for ever in the radiance of His Glory! Of this final Beatitude Communion gave her a foretaste, but only a foretaste, an incomplete joy, . . . mixed with desire.

It is the same with us; the more fervent our communions are, the better they make us understand, the more they make us desire the beatific vision.

Herself a model for the communicant, Mary has a special tenderness towards those who communicate frequently.

When she assisted at the agapes, what loving glances she gave the guests! Were they not the disciples, the admirers, the friends of Jesus? They tried to think, to feel, to act as He did. Each one of them was, for her, a Christ in the making, a future Jesus. They all had a family likeness, and the greater this resemblance, the more Mary loved them.

But when they had partaken of the consecrated Bread, it was no longer merely a likeness to Jesus that she saw in them; it was Jesus Himself. They were living tabernacles. Therefore, at the solemn instant of Communion,

Mary made no distinction, so to say, between them and her Divine Son; she included them in the same tender embrace with Him.

On their side, the first Christians were full of veneration for her in whom they saw the living image of Christ, the same features, the same way of looking, the same heavenly expression of countenance. And who knew Jesus better than His Mother? They, indeed, had followed Him, listened to Him, admired Him during His Public Life. But what He had said and done during His childhood and boyhood, no one knew better than His Mother. Oh! what would they not have given to enter that treasure-house of memories which Mary guarded so preciously . . . her heart! And how they must have wished that they could receive Him with that spirit of faith, that whole-heartedness that shone in her face, her attitude, her whole person.

Lively gratitude was mingled with their admiration. Through Mary this gift of God had been transmitted to them. It was thanks to her that they were able to taste this Bread of Life. The Second Body which nourished their souls was born of her. When she invited the faithful to the agape, she might have said: "Come, my children, eat the Bread and drink the Wine that I have prepared for you," *Venite, comedite panem meum et bibite vinum*

The Mother of Jesus

quod miscui vobis. We call her "Mother of Divine Grace": she is such, in fact, since she gave to the world the Author of supernatural life and the food that sustains it.

Like the early Christians, we associate the cult of the Blessed Virgin with that of the Eucharist. To the side of the Main Altar, where the Blessed Sacrament is generally reserved in our times and country, there is nearly always an altar dedicated to Mary. At Eucharistic Congresses, after the homage paid to Jesus in the Sacred Host, one feels impelled to thank and acclaim His Mother; witness the pilgrims to the Carthage Congress, who, at Cardinal Lépicier's invitation, closed the procession of the Blessed Sacrament by a hymn to the Blessed Virgin.

This connection is so natural that it has always existed in the Christian soul. François Villon in one of his poems, makes the delicious blunder of "the Virgin carrying the Sacrament they celebrate at Mass!" In the Middle Ages the Holy Reserve was contained in a silver dove which was itself enclosed in a tower suspended above the Choir. Did not the ingenious symbolism of our forefathers see in this tower an image of the Virgin bearing in her womb the Incarnate Word? Did they not associate the mystery of Christmas and the mystery of the Eucharist as the liturgy invites us to do?

156

After their example, we shall not put asunder what God has joined together. The Birth of Jesus, His Redemptive Death, the Sacrifice of the Altar renewing that of the Cross, are closely linked in the Christian economy, and to venerate as we ought any one of these mysteries, we must bear the others in mind.

We read in the life of St. Hyacinth that when the city where he lived was set on fire by the Tartars, he took the Ciborium of his Church in one hand and a much-venerated Statue of Our Lady in the other, and fled through the conflagration to the River Dnieper, which he crossed on the ice that covered it. Thus through fire and water and swords he saved the two objects most precious to him. What a picture and what a lesson! In this world of ours, we are surrounded with perils for body and soul, . . . especially for the soul. What safe-guard have we? This two-fold devotion to Mary and to the Holy Eucharist. Could Mary ever abandon those who, by Holy Communion, form but one with her Divine Son? And will the Sovereign Judge condemn those whom His Mother protects beneath her mantle?

XXI

CRUCIFIED WITH JESUS

MARY'S Cross was in proportion to her supernatural sanctity, her dignity as Mother of God, her rôle of Co-Redemptrix. The fact that her suffering was wholly moral, makes it none the less real, none the less poignant. The soul is as much in what it loves as in the body it animates. Identified with Jesus by sympathy, Mary felt His every torture, all His agony. In a very true sense, she was crucified with Him.

When one of the Apostles, John doubtless, came after the arrest of Jesus to give Mary the grim news, what a blow it was to her heart! She felt indeed the sword-thrust predicted thirty-three years before by Simeon. The Passion had already begun. Jesus was entering upon a road where every sort of pain was to fall upon Him and crush Him.

Mingled with the crowd, Mary beheld Him on the terrace of the Pretorium, but in what a state! Upon His head, a crown of thorns; in His bound hands, a sceptre of derision; over His shoulders, a rag from a soldier's red cloak,

158

which scarcely hid the wounds from the flagellation. "Behold the man!" cried the Roman Governor, exhibiting Him to His accusers. And the Virgin murmured: "Behold the Son of God, and this is how they treat Him! He is torn by scourges, mocked and derided by those He came to save!"

When the craven Pilate, fearing to be denounced to Rome and tired of defending an obscure Jew, had signed the sentence of death, the populace howled their triumph, and Mary uttered a moan of horror. An icy shadow fell upon her. It was finished then. Jesus had but a few hours to live!

In a narrow by-way, under the blazing sun, she saw Him again, bending beneath His Cross, the bill of His condemnation hanging from His neck, pushed and buffeted by the soldiers, hissed and hooted by the rabble. Turning towards Mary His livid face streaked with bloody welts, Jesus gave her a long, steady look. Mary's eyes were fixed upon Him, and this gaze, full of mutual compassion, was like a sharp dart transpiercing both.

At the foot of Calvary, she heard from afar the blows of the hammers, and the groans of the meek victim. Then the Cross emerged above the heads of the crowd, bearing that body she had pressed in her arms and to her heart. It was already as inert, as motionless as a corpse. The agony of the crucifixion had exhausted His strength. Jesus seemed not to see the mouths distorted with rage, the eyes blazing with hatred, the fists shaken against Him.

As the odious rabble dispersed, the group of Friends drew nearer to the Cross. Mary is now beside her Beloved. Long and intently she gazes at that Body, now one great wound, . . . that sanctuary of the Divinity ravaged and desecrated in a few hours!

The crown of Mary's sorrows is her helplessness. "I thirst!" He murmurs from the Cross, and she may not refresh His parched lips. She may not wipe away the blood dripping from His wounds! Oh! the martyrdom of a Mother who sees her beloved child in agony and can do nothing to relieve Him!

Knowing that His Mother's heaviest grief is the perspective of her desolate loneliness without Him, Jesus gives her a substitute, another Himself. "Woman," He says, designating St. John by a glance, "Behold thy son." The nearer He draws to the end of His earthly life, the more He discloses the loving thoughtfulness of His Divine Heart. The greater also grows Mary's tenderness, the deeper her anguish at the thought of losing Him.

As soon as Joseph of Arimathea had obtained permission, Jesus is taken down from the Cross. His poor body, begrimed with dust, soiled with sweat and blood, is reverently washed . . . cautiously, as though He could still suffer, the crown of thorns is removed. Then they proceed to a summary embalming. They have to hurry, because it is the eve of the Great Sabbath, and the Law forbids any work after sunset. Before Jesus is shrouded in the folds of the winding-sheet, Mary takes one last, long look at Him, and her heart breaks in the farewell kiss.

But it is after the Sepulchre is closed and sealed that the full meaning of her loss rushes upon her mind and heart. The Son Whom she has just been holding in her arms, . . . is gone, . . . she no longer has Him, . . . between Him and her rises that huge stone, lugubrious symbol of the separation between the living and the dead. Their mutual relations are severed; they are no longer in the same world.

The holy women share Mary's anguish. Leaning their foreheads against the stone sepulchre, they lament and weep, mourning for the Lord. For a long time this heart-rending wailing breaks the evening silence. The darkness of the Ninth Hour has not yet entirely disappeared. Below the black sky stretches what looks like a streak of blood. Everything is mourning in nature and in souls.

At last the Apostle John leads Mary away to his house.

The Mother of Jesus

But his affectionate devotion can not replace Him she has lost. The son of Zebedee is not the Son of God. And like Rachel bewailing her children on the hills of Rama, Mary would not be comforted because He was not.

The next day was the Feast of the Pasch. In all the streets groups of men, draped in their Sabbath mantles, were going to the Temple. They were going to lift in prayer their hands still red with blood! Oh! the smug satisfaction of these deicides! How it wounded!

Having considered what Mary suffered, let us now see how she bore these sorrows.

During His Passion the words of Jesus were few and brief. As for Mary, her silence seems to have been absolute. In circumstances as tragic as hers, the soul retires into itself: what lamentation could equal such grief!

Mary does not wring her hands, no gesture escapes her, she makes no reply to the invectives and challenges of the Pharisees. She preserves her calmness, her dignity, and, I would add, the beautiful attitude that befits the Mother of God.

The Gospel tells us that she stood at the foot of the cross. She stood: then she was not fainting, unconscious, prostrated, as several painters, more concerned with the effect of their work than with historical accuracy, have represented her. Firm, courageous, she mastered her emotions and did her duty to the end.

Throughout this terrible ordeal, her faith remained intact. When they beheld their Master nailed to the cross, several disciples doubted Him. What sort of King of Israel was this, Whose only throne was a gibbet? But the Virgin Mary relied upon the word of God and was not perturbed by such contingencies. Her faith never wavered for one instant. In this tortured man, agonizing upon a gallows, she saw the Messias, the Son of God.

What upheld her also was the thought that she was collaborating in a great work. She could not, of course, comprehend to its full extent, its whole depth, the mystery of Redemption. But with no will but the will of Jesus, she united herself to Him in intention. She offered Him to the Father and herself with Him. These two victims were so alike, so intimately united by ties of blood and affection, that in God's eyes they were but one.

On Calvary Mary endured a cruel torture. We should not, however, picture her suffering as an ocean of bitterness unrelieved by any sunbeam. She was happy in doing God's Will, in contributing to the execution of His Redemptive plan. As the new Eve, she was giving birth in pain to a new humanity. She foresaw the coming Resurrection and the Exaltation of Him Whom they had cruci-

163

fied. What matters a short period of agony, if, at that price, one can save the world!

Mary's example teaches us patience. The world has little use for this virtue. Yet there is none more practical and more suitable for daily use. No one has yet found nor ever will find any means of living without suffering. Pain will visit us often. Sorrow comes to us without warning, without asking leave. How are we to greet this guest or this intruder? Must we repulse her in anger, endure her with resignation, or embrace her with love?

The true Christian will not hesitate in his choice of these three attitudes. He will see in sorrow a messenger from God, and will revere it as he reveres Him Who sends it. Then sorrow will be transfigured, the repulsive aspect she wore at first will fade away and she will seem gracious and lovable.

Believing he had done good service to his country devastated by foreign and civil war, a poet exclaimed: "I have done my duty. All is well; I am happy to suffer." Is it then possible to find joy in suffering? Yes, experience proves it every day. We see it in the disciples of Jesus; their sorrow was turned into joy. Who is the magician who works this astonishing metamorphosis? It is Love.

After her husband's death a valiant Christian wrote:

"Do you know what hurts? It is resistance to sorrow. When one has once consented lovingly to everything, it does not matter much what the good pleasure of the Master holds in reserve for us. Everything is changed into acts of love, and thereby into joy." [1]

It was in these dispositions that Mary accepted the most excruciating suffering a mother's heart could endure. The God Who strikes is the same as the God Who gives: always infinitely good. Looking at His Love and not at His severity, Mary abandoned herself to Him wholly. May this admirable example teach us the art of suffering!

[1] Mireille Dupoucy.

XXII

THE QUEEN OF APOSTLES

IN THE Litany of the Blessed Virgin, we invoke her, and with good reason, as Queen of Apostles. Not only does she surpass them in dignity, but she is an admirable model for them. Her example shows us the source of zeal, and also in what conditions and by what means it must be exercised.

The source of zeal is evidently charity. Whoever loves God with all his heart thinks only of pleasing Him. Now the Will of God is that all men should be saved, and that they should come to the knowledge of the truth. It was for that end that Christ suffered, multiplied miracles, founded His Church. To work for the sanctification and salvation of souls is, therefore, to enter into His designs, and to give Him an irrefutable proof of our love.

Men living in society are like communicating vessels. Pour in a liquid and it will stand at the same level in each, whatever be its shape or capacity. We feel uncomfortable when persons with whom we live or associate do not share our sentiments. Equilibrium is disturbed, disagreement is introduced; we should like to restore the first and dispel the second.

If this be true, how Mary must have suffered to see her Divine Son misunderstood, hated, persecuted! He had resolute partisans, devoted friends; but how many were indifferent or actively hostile! Even among His relatives, some did not believe in Him; and those whose prejudices He jarred, whose pride He hurt, whose interests He endangered, bore Him deadly hatred. The Son of God had come unto His own, to the men who belonged to Him by so many titles; He had come unto His own, and His own received Him not. It was a disorder, an injustice, that Mary found difficult to bear. If she had yielded to the impulse of her heart, she would have gone through the hamlets of Palestine, crying like St. Francis of Assisi: "Love is not loved!"

"I live, now not I," said St. Paul, *"but Christ liveth in me."* This presence of Christ in us is not inactive. He fashions us to His own image; He inspires us with the sentiments of His great soul, especially zeal. The Apostle wrote to the Philippians: "I love you all in the heart of Christ," and again, elsewhere: "The charity of Christ urgeth us . . . It is God who exhorteth you by my mouth." St. Paul is as though out of himself, not his own property, . . . He looks upon himself as an instrument,

167

or rather, as an organ of Christ, Who lends him His Heart, His lips, His hands, with which to love, to preach, to work.

After the Ascension, more than ever, Mary experienced this intimate union, I might even venture to call it identification with Christ. She was only apparently separated from Him, since He lived in her and animated her by His spirit. He communicated to her His immense charity, His compassion for souls in danger of being lost. It is thus that she became the Refuge of Sinners, the Mother of Mercy.

In fervent Christians, especially mystics, love takes the form of gratitude. They constantly repeat with the Psalmist: "What shall I render to the Lord for all that He hath rendered unto me?" They are not able to make any adequate return and their inability distresses them. "To receive so much and to give nothing, what torment!" exclaimed St. Teresa.

These words reveal one aspect of Mary's interior life. No creature was ever so favored as she. And whence came her privileges, her Immaculate Conception, her perfect sanctity, her immense glory, if not from her divine maternity? It was because of Jesus that grace upon grace was showered upon her. And what can she give Him in return? Unable to add anything to His perfections or to

His Beatitude, she has but one means to show her gratitude: to win souls for Him. Her zeal is ardent, because she makes no distinction between love of God and love of mankind. She loves the whole Christ, i.e., her Divine Son together with all the faithful incorporated with Him in His Mystical Body. The natural Christ is perfect; but His Mystical Body can grow; this is a joy for Mary, because she can help to add new members to it until it has reached its full stature. To serve the Church and to serve Jesus is one and the same thing for her.

If one wishes to exercise the Apostolate, one must first know Christ, and who knew Him better than Mary?

She was His first disciple, and none understood His teachings better; but she especially penetrated herself with His spirit. Now spirit is propagated by common life still more than by word. To train a novice, one does not confine oneself to commenting the Rule; one puts him into contact with experienced religious. Seeing them in action, he absorbs little by little the spirit and as it were, the tone of the Institute. A soul kindles by contact with a soul, as a torch is lighted by another torch. That is why the Divine Educator kept His disciples with Him for three whole years. But what was that Noviceship compared to the hidden life? For thirty years Mary lived

169

under the eye of the Man-God, and like a clear crystal she was filled with His light.

Her lively tenderness increased still more her clear-sightedness. A medieval theologian, Richard of St. Victor, says very aptly that to love is to see. *Amare videre est, amor oculus est.* The more tender our affection, the keener our perspicacity.

That Mary possessed this intuitive faculty, this gift of second-sight, is sufficiently proved by the incident of Cana. To His Mother's request, Jesus replied with apparent curtness: "My hour is not yet come." But Mary knows how to interpret His words: she hears "yes" when Jesus seems to say "no"; and foreseeing the miracle about to be wrought, she advises the waiters: "Whatsoever He shall say to you, do ye."

Notice also that the Mother of Jesus was the principal witness of the scenes of His Childhood. When St. Matthew and St. Luke undertook to relate them, everything leads us to think that they had recourse to her. Mary was then in her own way the Doctor of the Evangelists.

But it is above all by prayer, by suffering and by example that she promoted the interests of her Divine Son. The holier a soul is the greater is her power of intercession. What then must Mary's power be! God will refuse her nothing!

According to St. Paul's expression, she also "filled up in her flesh what was wanting to the sufferings of Christ." What then was lacking to the sufferings of Christ? Our own! Since we were lost by our own fault, it is not just that we should be saved without our co-operation. Our works of satisfaction bear assuredly no proportion to the gravity of our offences, infinite in some sort, since they offend the infinite Majesty of God. But is not the insolvent debtor bound to pay what he can? And as most men neglect this plain duty, divine justice would not be satisfied unless generous souls paid for them. The Queen of Martyrs was one of these voluntary victims. As she herself had no need of expiation, her merits were deposited in the treasury of the Church and contributed to the ransom of humanity.

Finally by her example, she edified those who had the happiness to approach her. Contrary to the Law of Gravitation, the ideal has greater power to attract the further it is removed. A single act of heroism will galvanize a battalion more than a hundred deeds of ordinary courage. Hence the social value of Holiness. Like a mighty magnet it lifts the masses, or at least prevents their slipping down too low. Mary's holiness was extremely attractive because she was perfect. No one could converse with her, nay, even gaze upon her, without feeling nearer to God.

The influence of her example was not merely external; it sanctified souls in a mysterious manner, of which the apostolate of St. Thérèse of Lisieux gives us some idea. During a religious ceremony, she watched one of her sisters approach a lamp to light a candle. The candle flame was then used to light all the candles the religious were holding, so that the Chapel which had been almost dark a minute before, was brilliantly illuminated. Thérèse said to herself: "Thus the Carmelite is consumed before the altar like a tiny flame; but the charity which is burning her up is communicated to the whole Church. She is the Apostle of the Apostles."

Was the little Saint right? One might believe it, if one recalls the doctrine of the Mystical Body: *"When one member suffers,"* says St. Paul, *"all the other members suffer with it."* When virtue, piety, faith, decline in one single Christian, the whole Church is impoverished by that much. When one member grows stronger, all the others benefit by the increase of strength. "One soul that rises, lifts the world," says Elizabeth Leseur.

To make Christ known, the apostle makes use of two principal means: he speaks of Him, he *lives* Him. Of the two, the second is by far the more efficacious. It is precisely because Mary had saturated herself with the spirit of the Gospel, and radiated it in her speech, in her conduct, in her whole person, that she is the model and the Queen of Apostles.

Let us beg the grace to be, like her, living Ostensoriums, to cultivate in ourselves a permanent reflection of the Divine Beauty, to live the Gospel in order to make it loved. If we show Jesus to men on earth, Mary will one day show Him to us in Heaven, where, gathered together around her we shall be eternally happy in loving and admiring Him.

XXIII

The Virgin and Saint John

AFTER the drama of Calvary, St. John took to his own abode her who by the Will of Christ had become his second mother. According to tradition he took a son's care of her for about fifteen years. Let us meditate upon this intimacy full of sweetness and mystery.

"When two or three of you shall be gathered together in My name, I shall be in the midst of you." This promise of Christ was fulfilled in a marvelous way for Mary and St. John. In their dwelling, which was like a new House of the Holy Family, a new sanctuary of hidden life, one felt the presence of an invisible Host.

They often spoke of Him. Recollections of youth become extremely lively with the decline of age. Mary took pleasure in describing the scenes of Jesus' Childhood, in recalling words that had struck her. It was a joy to her to evoke these charming memories which she alone possessed. On his side, St. John, whose eagle eye had pierced the veil and gazed into divine depths, shared with Mary the revelations with which he had been favored. They put their lights in common, and when the name of Jesus was not on their lips, it was in their hearts; their thoughts returned to Him as the magnetic needle seeks its pole.

Jesus was present also in resemblance. It is probable that St. John had a family likeness to Him, since his mother, Salome, was a relative of the Blessed Virgin. If Jesus loved John more than the other apostles, it was because John had most thoroughly imbibed His spirit. Amongst all his works the artist prefers that in which he has put most of himself, the one that best expresses his ideal. As to Mary, she was at once the disciple and Mother of Jesus. God had dowered her with the qualities and the virtues which, by the law of heredity, she was to pass on to her divine Son. Formed on the same model, Mary and St. John resembled each other, they were two living portraits of the same original.

It was for love's sake that Jesus gave them to each other. For thirty years He had been for Mary the most respectful, the most obedient, the most loving of all sons. After His Resurrection, He continued to love her, but His filial piety no longer manifested itself in a sensible way. Therefore He chose a substitute, who would show His Mother the consideration He Himself had shown, and it was John whom He called to this signal honor. He bequeathed to the Virgin Apostle, the only Apostle who had remained with Him in His agony, the dearest treasure He possessed. Could He have given him a more distinguished mark of confidence and friendship?

It was for love of His friend and of His Mother that He associated them in a common life; it was also on His account that they loved each other. St. John revered Mary to please Him Who had confided her to his solicitude. Mary is so wholly one with her divine Son, that she wants everything He wants.

It is true that she can not help an occasional mental comparison between the Master and the disciple, between the Son of God and the son of Zebedee. John's delicate kindness is extreme; but he is not Jesus. The incomparable One, the Only One is no longer at her side. To realize this revives all the anguish of the Passion. St. John guesses the thoughts of his adoptive Mother, and as though to entreat her pardon for not being Jesus, he is doubly attentive and loving. He would like to be a Jesus for her sake.

This moral presence, by thought, by resemblance, by love, becomes a real Presence in the Eucharist. There is a picture representing Mary and St. John seated at a small table. It is the end of the family agape; the Apostle, mindful of the words: "Do this in commemoration of Me," takes bread, lifts his eyes to heaven, and pronounces the mysterious and potent words: "This is My Body." From the consecrated Bread streams a bright light, in this supernatural brightness angelic forms appear. Mary, her eyes fixed upon the Host, holds out her hands. She can not wait for her adoptive son, her priest, the first Chaplain of Our Lady, to give her the Body of her true Son, of her Jesus. It is not difficult to imagine the scene which must have followed. Mary and St. John with clasped hands and bowed heads, rapt in prayer, lost in the recollection of a silent and delightful thanksgiving. Oh! how each must have lived over again the blessed hours passed in the visible companionship of the most beautiful of the sons of men! Oblivious of each other, of themselves, of all else, they are absorbed in Him. Both make but one in Christ Jesus!

Spiritual life is a dual life. It is Christ living in us Who renders our prayers efficacious, our good works and our sufferings meritorious. He is the soul of our soul, our second soul. What is true of us is equally true of our brethren in the faith. When it is said that Christians have but one soul, it does not mean merely the same beliefs, the same feelings; this expression *anima una* signifies that they have a common principle of spiritual life: they are the branches which derive from the same stem the life-giving sap.

Thus the Blessed Virgin and St. John felt themselves intimately united to Christ. The roots of their being were deeply sunk in common soil; and like two violin strings vibrating under the same bow, they sang in unison the joy of believing, of hoping, of loving.

Living *by* Jesus, they live *for* Him also. Each in a personal, individual way worked His work. John meditated, wrote, preached. He founded and administered churches. His ministry obliged him to make long and frequent absences. When he was away, Mary helped him by her prayers; on his return she lavished care and attentions upon him to rest him after his labors. She played the same part as the holy women, Susanna, Joanna, and Mary of Magdala had done, who during His Public Life followed the Divine Preacher and provided for His needs. It was Jesus Whom Mary saw and served in the person of His disciple.

How often we have admired in the Confessions of St. Augustine the scene he describes on the sea-shore at Ostia. He and his mother St. Monica are seated side by side, hand in hand, but they are not looking at each other. Beyond this world, beyond all things sensible, they gaze

178

upward, and like two converging lines, their ardent glances meet in the infinite.

One loves to picture Mary and St. John praying thus in the still evening on the terrace of their house. Beyond the soft sky of the Orient, where the first stars are twinkling, they seek another heaven, more beautiful far. Jesus is in them, but an impenetrable veil conceals Him from their sight. Oh! for the moment when death shall draw the veil aside and disclose to them His adorable Face! They long to die that they may be with Christ. One and the same aspiration uplifts and carries them out of themselves, they might be saying: "O Jesus! I am Thine, I am going to Thee! Heaven . . . it is Thou, my Jesus!"

Death did not interrupt the relations of St. John and the Blessed Virgin. If they are saved, the dead live in God, Who is, as we have said, the "locus" of souls; they are therefore, only seemingly separated. After the Assumption, the Seer of Patmos frequently turned his thoughts to his adoptive Mother. He speaks of her in the Apocalypse. She appeared to him one day in the form of a Woman clothed with the sun, a magnificent image of Mary's glory which comes to her entirely from her relations with Jesus. It is therefore just that she should be enthroned beside Him there above, enveloped in His aureola, living, in some sort, in the shining of the Sun of Justice.

How many lessons we may learn from so wonderful an example! It teaches us first of all that God always mingles consolation with trial. When Christ enters into His glory, He has to leave His Mother. But knowing how sorely she would miss Him in solitude, He leaves her a friend, a son, another Himself. He remains close to her, hidden under the appearances of the Host. He acts, He lives in her by His grace. He comforts her by the hope of eternal and beatific communion in Heaven.

And we, if we cast a look upon the past, will see that there has not been a day so dark as not to be brightened by one ray from above. God, Who promises heaven to those who visit the sick for His sake, visits us also in our afflictions. Happy those wise enough to recognize Him!

The intimacy of the Blessed Virgin and St. John reveals to us also the excellence of Christian friendship. It is not an association for pleasure or interest, a contract for mutual adoration, a double egotism. It has been very justly defined as Christ between two souls. True friends seek each other because each sees in the other an image of Christ, and they collaborate with Him in the same work. Their affection is most pure. Beauty of feature is for them but the manifestation of moral beauty. In the eye, the smile, the tone of the voice, it is the soul they seek, and through the soul, Him Who made it. Their affection, inspired by

God, rises to Him again as the sunbeam, reflected from the surface of our globe, returns to the source whence it came.

And let it not be imagined that this spiritual friendship is a chilly, languid sentiment. Transported to the supernatural plane, our feelings become at once both purer and livelier. Let us implore the grace to love thus, reciting the admirable prayer of St. John Eudes:

"O Heart of Jesus, since the Father of Mercy and God of all consolation has given Thee to me in giving me Jesus, and Thou art truly in my heart, love Thou for me all those that I should love, and in the way that God wishes me to love them."

XXIV

THE TRIUMPH OF MARY

IN A Breton Chapel that bears the graceful name: Our Lady of the Flowers, one may admire a large stained glass window representing the Assumption. The Apostles are grouped around the open tomb in which miraculous flowers are wafting fragrance from their opening corollas. But the Blessed Virgin is there no longer; she has left as a witness to her passage these lilies, whose purity, fragrance, freshness and color symbolize so well the beauty of her soul. And the Apostles, remembering the day of the Ascension, lift their eyes to heaven, longing to see once more the Virgin whom they reverenced as the living image of Jesus.

We, too, love to raise our eyes to the starry throne whence Mary, herself the most brilliant star, looks down and blesses her adoptive children. But while our hearts rejoice in her triumph, our minds, always seeking the causes of things, wonder how she merited this triumph. At the general resurrection, our bodies will again be united to our souls to share their eternal destiny. But why has

Mary passed ahead of us? what are her claims to this signal honor?

It is a dogma of faith that Mary was preserved from original sin, and consequently from concupiscence (i.e., inordinate desires) from the first instant of her conception. Her purity was perfect, absolute.

This privilege, which was conferred on her at the beginning of her life, called for a corresponding, a congruous or fitting privilege, at its close. God Almighty had said to our first parents: "Because you have violated My Law, you shall die the death." In the execution of this sentence, the body has first to be separated from the soul and then destroyed. It must be, because it seduces us to evil, it is sinful flesh, and for Satan, it is an instrument by which he reigns. Therefore God allows it to crumble into dust, in order to reconstruct it, as one lets a dilapidated house fall down when one plans to rebuild.

But the Blessed Virgin's body was perfectly pure, there was no reason why she should be subject to the universal law. She had to die, for Christ Himself died for the salvation of the world. But death is one thing, decomposition is another. It was not fitting that the Body of Jesus, that Sanctuary of the Divinity should know the corruption of the grave. It was not fitting either that the virginal flesh of Mary should disintegrate. Therefore, shortly after she had breathed her last sigh, her soul resumed possession of her body. Once more she saw the light of day, and death was for her "but the twinkling of an eyelid which does not interrupt vision."

If Mary was the first to rise from the dead, there is another reason: she was the first to receive Communion. We know from the Gospel that the Eucharist is a pledge of a glorious Resurrection. When in the synagogue of Capharnaum Jesus announced His intention to institute this Sacrament: "He who eateth My Flesh," He said, "hath everlasting life, and I shall raise him up on the last day."

The primitive Church was permeated with this teaching, and its belief has left traces. Archeologists have recently made an interesting discovery in Palestine. In a Christian grave of the first centuries, they found a sort of terra-cotta dish, where in a cavity covered by glass a perfectly recognizable Host could be seen. They inferred from this that it was the custom at that period to place a consecrated Host in the tomb. Elsewhere a Host was placed in the mouth of the deceased. This custom, which rightly shocks us, was condemned by the Church, but abuse as it was in itself, it was an indication of real faith. The early Christians whose faith was so lively and literal, recalled the words of Christ cited above, and that is why they placed a consecrated Host either beside the deceased or on his lips, as though to say: "According to the general Law this flesh shall perish, but not for ever. It is not possible that this Christian flesh, flesh of a communicant, . . . this body that has been consecrated and divinized, so to say, by contact with the adorable Flesh of Jesus Christ, should be plunged into corruption for ever! No! the triumph of death is but for a time. It reduces the body to its elements and scatters them; but God will collect the fragments of this shattered ciborium and make of them a vessel of election, precious and incorruptible!"

Thus the Eucharist gives us a right to resurrection. Now Mary was the first communicant. You are perhaps familiar with the picture representing her receiving Communion from the hand of St. John. She is kneeling on the step of a small altar. St. John, in alb and ample chasuble, is laying the Sacred Host upon her lips, while beyond the arcade opening a wide view over the country-side, angels are contemplating the scene with rapture. It is a ravishing scene, indeed, and worthy to inspire the greatest artist: Mary, assisting at the Mass of her adoptive son and receiving from him the Body of her true Son, of her Jesus.

But this Communion, which she must so often have repeated, was not her first. If one understands by "communion" the intimate union of the Incarnate Word with a human person, one must admit that the first of all communions took place at Nazareth, on the day of the Annunciation. When Gabriel had asked Mary if she consented to become the Mother of God and she replied: *Fiat mihi secundum verbum tuum,* the mystery of the Incarnation took place at once. Instantaneously the Word of God was made flesh in her virginal womb. She really and truly received the body and blood, soul and divinity of Jesus Christ. She became a living tabernacle. And you behold the consequences. Since the Holy Eucharist is a pledge of glorious resurrection, and Mary was the first communicant, it was fitting that she should be the first to rise again. God did not permit that her virginal body, the source of the Redeemer's Blood, should become the prey of corruption; and as soon as she had expired He took up to Heaven this first tabernacle of the Incarnate Word.

But Mary's chief title to immediate resurrection was her dignity as Mother of God.

When death has robbed us of some one dear to us, we can not at once realize our loss. For weeks afterwards, we are confused and bewildered. It seems as though he were near, observing our actions, divining our thoughts, coming to us in dreams. Is it an illusion? Probably; but Christians who are very learned and very orthodox are not far from believing that it is a reality. Some months after the death of his dearly-loved mother, Frédéric Ozanam wrote: "There come instants when I am suddenly startled as if she were there at my side; there are hours, especially when I most need it, of mother-and-son communings; and then I weep, more perhaps than during the first months, but with the sadness there mingles an ineffable peace. When I am good, when I have done something for the poor she loved so much, when I am at peace with God Whom she served so well, I see her smiling on me from afar. Sometimes, when I am praying, I think I hear her praying with me, as we used to pray together in the evening before the crucifix. . . . And then I firmly believe in the real presence of my mother beside me."

However it may be with the reality of this posthumous presence, it does not satisfy us, real though it be. We need to see those we love, to have intercourse with them.

Now, do you think that Christ, true God and true Man, did not feel this yearning so natural and so legitimate? His Heart beat like ours, only more strongly. In virtue of its union with the Divinity, all the faculties of His human nature, including sensitiveness, were carried to their highest power. We have noticed in reading the Bible the extreme vivacity of His emotions. What indignation against the Pharisees! What affection for St. John! What impetuous desire! How impatient He is to die for men and to give Himself as their food!

What is true of His other feelings, is equally true of His filial piety. No one ever loved a mother as Jesus loved His. But, unlike ours, His love was served by omnipotence.

One of our poets, Sully-Prudhomme, wrote:

> If I were God, for thee, O my Beloved!
> The sky should be for ever clear and blue!

He might have added: "If I were God, I'd keep thee ever at my side!"

But what for us is only a wish, a dream, is easily accomplished by the God-Man. Nothing prevented Him from fully satisfying His filial love. Therefore, no sooner had Mary ended her life on earth, than He said to her in the words of Holy Writ inspired by Himself: "Winter is now past. The rain is over and gone. Arise, make haste, My love, My dove, My beautiful one, and come!"

At these words, Mary opens her eyes. Celestial harmony greets her. Invisible hands, most pure and gentle, lift her, and behold! she rises to Heaven as swiftly as lightning flashes from the sky.

What were her sensations when she made her entrance into the Father's House, acclaimed by the angelic choirs? Let us not attempt to imagine! These are matters that exceed our powers. We may, however, suppose that on the day of her Assumption, Mary remembered the Canticle she had composed in her youth in Elizabeth's house. Her triumph was the consequence of her Divine Maternity, and must have inspired her with the same emotions of joy, enthusiasm, and humble gratitude. "My soul doth magnify the Lord, and my spirit hath rejoiced in God, my Saviour. Because He that is mighty hath done great things in me and holy is His name. Because He hath regarded the humility of His Handmaid, for behold from henceforth all generations shall call me blessed!"

A magnificent vision, certainly, and a very comforting one for us. In order to confirm our faith in the general resurrection and to prove to us that He will keep His promise, Jesus began by His Mother. What He has done for her He will do also for us. On beautiful summer evenings, when we prolong our enjoyment of the fresh, cool air, we love to watch the stars come out. First one appears, shining like a pearl in the fading blue, then another, and another, until the sky is all a-twinkle with constellations. Well! in the supernatural order we shall behold a similar spectacle. Jesus and Mary have risen already, and shine on the heights of Heaven like two glorious suns. They went first to prepare a place for us. But one day we shall join them, if we have the happiness of dying in the state of grace. We shall take our places beside them, and then shall be fulfilled for us the words of the Scriptures: "the just shall shine like the sun under the eye of God."

XXV

STELLA MATUTINA

ONE of our poets describes in the following words the radiant Morning Star:

I fell asleep last night upon the beach;
A chill breeze woke me, scattering my dream;
Op'ning my eyes, I saw the Morning Star,
Shining resplendent, high, deep-set and far
In a soft whiteness, magic, infinite,
The brilliant star had changed the cloud to down,
A brightness that pulsated, lived—nay, thought,—
A soul, it seemed, seen through a lustrous pearl.[1]

Is this not an image of humanity before the Redemption? It was languishing in darkness. Then, lo! a mysterious brightness pierces the clouds, a star appears, heralding the dawn. The sky is illumined by a divine smile. Hope revives in men's hearts. Well may they rejoice! Mary is born; their Deliverer is near!

If we invoke the Blessed Virgin under the title of Morning Star, it is because she was the fore-runner of the

[1] Victor Hugo, *Stella*.

The Mother of Jesus

Messias, the Dawn of the Sun of Justice, or, as Bossuet says: "the Christ-begun." But this is not the only reason. Between Mary and the Star that is the harbinger of day there are numerous and striking analogies.

Like the star, Mary is pure. When we seek symbols of perfect purity, we think of the snow on mountain peaks, untrodden by any foot, or else of the flame that burns and consumes anything thrown upon it that might defile its brightness. Now Mary is a bright and shining flame. She is all light. Like her divine Son, she could say: "In me the Demon has not anything," . . . nothing that resembles him, nothing that belongs to him.

It is not so with us, alas! Every man is a mixture of good and evil; a field in which cockle grows with the wheat. The devil lays hold of us by what St. Augustine calls "our garment of flesh," i.e., concupiscence. He pulls us and sometimes makes us trip or stumble. As we frequently fall, we must often beg pardon of God. Our soul can not otherwise maintain its purity. What we call "pure water" is filtered or distilled water; so a soul in the state of grace is a soul that has been cleansed from sin.

But the Blessed Virgin had no need of such purification. Preserved from original sin, exempt from concupiscence, Satan had no hold on her. Never did she commit the slightest fault, nay, more, never was she even tempted (in the strict sense of the term). She never knew some feelings quite habitual with us, such as repentance, or dread of falling into sin.

O perfect security of a soul confirmed in grace! O Lily of Purity, how we could envy thee!

Like the star, Mary is simple. Her spiritual wealth is inexhaustible. But all her virtues blend into one. They are potentially contained in the love of God, as the seven prismatic colors form white light.

Goodness is the basis of all natures august:
God formed of one virtue the heart of the just,
As of a single sapphire He shaped the vault of Heaven.[1]

Replace the word "Goodness" by charity, love, and these beautiful verses will be a portrait of Mary. They will remind you of the one source of all her qualities of mind and heart.

The complications of sinful souls come from their being at odds with themselves; they are pulled in opposite directions. If they love material goods more than spiritual, their lives are an uninterrupted succession of falls. They

[1] Victor Hugo.

go from disaster to disaster without losing their hope of heaven. They are like ship-wrecked mariners, who in their disabled, storm-tossed boat, stretch out their arms to the fast receding shore. A tragic situation surely! To love virtue, to aspire to everlasting happiness, and to let oneself drift, in one's own despite, into sin and eternal reprobation!

When love of God is stronger than love of the world, the soul falls only by surprise. It remains habitually in the state of grace, but not without a struggle. It is tempted, and has to make a violent effort, sometimes, to escape or withstand the formidable fascination of evil.

Mary never experienced this interior conflict. God is all to her. Her affections are but forms of her love. She never had to struggle with herself, to watch herself, to restrain herself, her first impulse was always towards the good. In this ideal creature, we admire at one and the same time, the purity of the Virgin, the loving goodness of the Mother, the heroism of the Saint, and also the candor, the divine spontaneity of the Child.

In appearance a star is but a golden point, but this point is a miniature universe. It would take thirteen hundred thousand globes like our earth to equal the volume of the sun; but the sun is but a star amongst the thousand-thousands of others. What marvels there are in every one of the stars whose delicate and gracious shining charms us at night!

There is the same contrast between Mary's humble condition on earth and her eminent dignity. During the days that followed the Annunciation, when she went to draw water at the well of Nazareth, nothing marked her off from her companions unless it were a greater modesty in deportment and speech. And yet a tremendous mystery had been accomplished in her. She bore in her inner tabernacle Him Whom the universe can not contain.

God never withdraws His gifts except to replace them with better. Before returning to Heaven, Jesus instituted the Eucharist, which is like an Incarnation continued, universalized, appropriated to each single one of us. More favored in one sense than were His contemporaries, who could only see and hear Him, we can also unite ourselves to Him intimately. Hence He could say to His Apostles saddened by His approaching departure: "It is expedient for you that I go."

He was not less generous to Mary. Having once given Himself to her, He gave Himself for ever. At the Last Supper on the eve of His Passion, He said to His Father: "I in them, and Thou in Me; that they may be made perfect in one." If Christ dwells in His disciples, how much more intimately does He not abide with His Mother! Since the Annunciation, He has always dwelt and will always dwell with her, in a manner mysterious but none the less real.

A ray of light leaving the spiral Nebula nearest to our globe takes about ten thousand centuries to reach us. This figure gives some idea of the enormous distance to which the stars project their light. Prodigious is their power of radiation, for they are themselves prodigious conflagrations.

What is true of stars is true also of persons. The more intense the love in their heart, the more love they radiate. Look at St. Thérèse of the Child Jesus. Her life was spent humbly and monotonously in the shadow of the cloister. And today her beneficent influence extends over the whole world. Why? Because she loved Jesus Christ with all the tenderness, all the enthusiasm of her virginal heart.

If the Blessed Virgin is today so glorious, so powerful, it is for the same reason. The ardor of her love is the measure of her power to radiate love. God refuses nothing to those who have given Him everything. Jesus does not forget that at Bethlehem He laid claim with cries and tears to His Mother's care and attention; can He resist her when she asks Him today to help her adoptive children? He will throw open His treasures to her, that she may distribute with lavish hand the succor needed by those who invoke her. Beholding this continuous outpouring of graces, is one not reminded of a meadow on a lovely Spring day? Every blade of grass is reaching for the sky, every flower is lifting up its chalice to the sun to catch its share of sunshine. Thus, from every corner of the earth the faithful turn to Mary, and the Mother of Mercy replies to each with that gentle look which fills souls with peace, consolation, hope.

Mary is also called the Star of the Sea, because she is our guide and our safeguard in the storms of life.

Before the discovery of the compass, mariners had nothing to indicate direction at night but a small star that shows the North, and is called the Pole Star. What dismay and distress when fog or tempest hid it from their sight! And what relief, what joy, when the sky was once more serene and the star visible, to see the star meant safety!

Devotion to Mary is a pledge of salvation. Not, of course, that a medal or a scapular are amulets which by any power of their own can preserve us from damnation. But the Blessed Virgin does obtain for those who have always honored her the grace of final perseverance. And how could one admire and honor her without esteeming her virtues, without feeling oneself attracted and uplifted by her example? It is safe to augur well for a Christian who sincerely loves the Blessed Virgin. He may be tempest-tossed, but he has a star in heaven that will guide him safe to port.

The ancients gave to stars the names of their gods and goddesses, and we still call the planets Venus, Mars, Mercury, Jupiter, etc. God forbid that the starry heavens should evoke for us nothing but pagan Mythology! Our faith should permeate everything, purify everything, even our feeling for nature. Let us look at the sky with Christian eyes, and we shall think of the Creator, Who, with one gesture scattered through space these billions of worlds; we shall think also of the Morning Star whose smiling brightness is the image and the promise of Heaven.

XXVI

SUPPLEMENT TO THE LITANIES

THE Litanies of the Blessed Virgin are one long exclamation of admiration. In love with the beauties of his Queen, the Christian is never weary of gazing upon her. She appears to him in ever new aspects; and to praise her numberless perfections, he multiplies the most vivid expressions, the most poetic images, Seat of Wisdom, House of Gold, Tower of Ivory, Morning Star.

In official prayer, it became necessary to moderate this gushing enthusiasm. But when the Litany comes to an end, the faithful continue interiorly. What has been said by no means exhausts all that could be said! He seeks new epithets!

He thinks of the Tree of Life planted in the Garden of Eden whose fruit would have rendered our first parents immortal, had they obeyed the divine Law. Thus the Blessed Virgin bore a delicious fruit. Whoever eats thereof is preserved from eternal death. "My flesh is meat indeed," said Jesus, "My blood is drink indeed. He that eateth My flesh and drinketh My blood hath everlasting life, and I shall raise him up on the last day."

It was Mary who prepared this food for us. It is she who formed in her virginal womb Him Whom we receive at the altar or the communion-rail. We may, therefore, call her Queen of the Holy Eucharist. Our Lady of the Blessed Sacrament. Each time we receive Holy Communion, let it be with a profound sentiment of gratitude to her who gave Jesus to the world. The Liturgy itself invites us not to separate devotion to the Holy Eucharist and devotion to the Blessed Virgin. The Church bids us sing before the Sacred Host: "Ave verum Corpus *natum de Maria Virgine* . . ." Hail, true Body born of the Virgin Mary!"

Jesus cried out in the Temple of Jerusalem, on the day of the great Libation: "Let him that thirsteth come unto Me, and I shall give him to drink." He is the Fountain of Life, but it is Mary who brings its waters to us. She, then, is the Channel of Grace. In countries once colonized by the Romans, it is not unusual to find ruined aqueducts. These channels once carried from the mountains the pure, fresh water and with it health to men and fruitfulness to the earth. Today the springs are still where they were, high up, in the mountain fastnesses; but the life-giving water no longer descends to the sun-baked plain below.

Sad image of individuals and peoples who no longer honor the Blessed Virgin. They have forgotten their Mother and are perishing for lack of care.

In his Treatise on the True Devotion to the Blessed Virgin, Blessed Grignon de Montfort calls Mary the Hall of the Divine Sacraments, where Jesus Christ and all the saints have been formed. It is from Christ that we have our concept of the world and of life, our moral ideal, our rule of conduct. Living in us, He enlightens our mind, touches our heart, strengthens our will. He fashions and shapes us

> Not as a modeler, whose agile thumb
> Runs round the plastic mass and presses out
> The shape that he with inward vision sees;
> But as that model, quickened into life,
>   Kneading himself the clay as he may please.[1]

We have been formed by Christ, but He Himself was formed by Mary, His Mother and His first teacher. The influence she exercised over Him has extended to all Christians. It is of her above all that it is true to say "The hand that rocks the cradle moves the world."

The Blessed de Montfort also calls Mary the Mould of God, the Echo of God. He says: "Mary is the great and

[1] Sully-Prudhomme, *La Justice*.

The Mother of Jesus

only Mould of God, fitted to turn out living images of God, without great expense and in a short time. A soul who has found this mould and cast herself into it, is soon changed into Jesus Christ, Whom this mould represents to the life. You never think of Mary, but she, in your place, thinks of God . . . Mary is wholly relative to God, and I would call her the Echo of God, who says and ever repeats only *God, God.*"

Hence it follows that Mary is the Mother of the Church. In bringing Jesus into the world, she, in a sense, founded the religious society that was to be born of Him. And since by Baptism we become members of a body of which Christ is the Head and the Life, . . . since we are, so to say, deified by this incorporation, Mary is the "Mother of God-made-Man and of Man-made-God."

Mary is the Terrestrial Paradise of the New Adam. Having come into the world to found a new humanity, the Word Incarnate lay in the womb and in the arms of Mary. He lived always at her side. His eyes, offended by so much moral ugliness, so much bad faith and bad will, rested with delight upon His Mother. Mary's soul was a pure and shining Temple in which His Name resounded ceaselessly in a canticle of praise. Ah! if He had reigned thus in all souls!

In his *Pensées Choisies* M. Olier compares Mary to

the Seven-Branched Candlestick, forty ells in height, that illuminated the Temple. She illuminates the Church; first, because she bore Him Who said: "I am the Light." She illuminates it in reflecting the Sun of Justice. No one ever better understood and practised the teachings of Jesus. No one more closely resembles Him. Whoever sees the Mother sees the Son. How happy is the soul that shares in her eminent sanctity! "O Jesus, living in Mary, in the beauty of Thy virtues, in the greatness of Thy power, in the splendor of Thy riches, grant us a share in that sanctity that unites her to God alone; communicate to us her zeal for the Church; clothe us all with Thyself, that we may be nothing in ourselves, that we may live solely as she does, for the glory of God."

Since Mary is wholly steeped in the spirit of the Gospel, and radiates this spirit in her speech, in all her actions, in her entire person, she manifests Jesus to men: she is a "monstrance," a Living Ostensorium.

Mary is the Gate of Heaven. It is through her that the Word Incarnate entered the world. It is through her that we shall enter eternal life. We read in St. Anselm, "Just as it is impossible for us to be saved without devotion to Mary, so it is impossible to be damned when one has recourse to the Blessed Virgin and she looks on us with love."

Mary is the Virgin-Priest. She fulfills eminently all the sacerdotal functions. As heavenly Mediatrix she presents our petitions to God and transmits His favors to us. She does not change bread into the Body of Christ; but it is she who formed that Body. She does not absolve sins, but she implores pardon for them. She does not preach the Gospel, but she exemplifies it in her person, and what more efficacious than this silent preaching!

> From a good book, a Christian may learn his duty ill,
> Examples that are living have greater power still.

Mary is like the Sealed Book of the Apocalypse. The whole life of Jesus is written therein. This priceless, incomparable, unique Book was carried to Heaven on the day of the Assumption; and that accounts for the incompleteness of our knowledge of Christ. Let us hope that it will soon be opened before our fascinated eyes! What wonders we shall see in it; what charming traits of character in Jesus; what words He said that have never been repeated; what scenes of the Divine Childhood known to Mary only, the memory of which is graven in her heart! What are our most precious volumes in comparison!

We should never finish if we had to enumerate all the titles that Catholic piety has bestowed on Mary. Some recall the countries and the sanctuaries or shrines where she is particularly honored: Our Lady of Puy, Our Lady of Paris, Our Lady of Chartres. Like titles of nobility, these are the names of her domains.

On August 15, 1638, Louis XIII consecrated himself and his Kingdom to Mary. Since that memorable day, Mary is the Queen of France. Between her and our country there are special relations; a sort of contract which puts France in a rank apart and confers upon it privileges bestowed upon no other. Needs there any other proof than the three Apparitions of the last Century, and the innumerable miracles registered at Lourdes!

Other titles relate to the prerogatives of Mary or to favors bestowed by her: Mother of the Living, New Eve, Queen of Hearts, Mother of Holy Love, Our Lady of Protection, Our Lady of Safety, Our Lady of Perpetual Help, Our Lady of Joy, Our Lady of Deliverance, Our Lady of All Help, Patroness of a Happy Death. How many titles of glory! How many gems in our Mother's Crown! But for her faithful lovers there are never enough!

Here is another one, full of promise for us: Queen of Heaven, Our Lady of Paradise. Ah! may we behold her one day on her throne all glittering with stars! We shall not need to recite Litanies then, nor to consider her perfections one after another; we shall see them all in one glance! We shall revel in her beauty, as pure and as simple as a white rose.

In Heaven our prayer will no longer be a stammering; it will be better than a discourse, however eloquent, better than a hymn, however ardent, for both these presuppose a succession of words, a series of thoughts that complete each other. No! it will be one long, intense look fixed upon the beauty of our Queen. This look will say to her: "O Mary, I venerate and love thee!" And Mary herself will look at her Divine Son as though she were saying, "It is Thou, Whom they are honoring in me. These myriads of elect, enchanted by a reflection of Thy light, these blessed ones ravished in a perpetual ecstasy, it is Thou Who hast saved and sanctified them. Their brows are signed with Thy mark. I offer Thee their homage, their love, their joy. To Thee be all honor and glory."

XXVII

BENEFITS OF DEVOTION TO MARY

"WHOEVER wants grace and has not recourse to Mary is trying to fly without wings," sings Dante. Mary is the Almoner of God, the Treasurer of Paradise. And not only does she obtain and transmit grace, but she purifies and sanctifies those who honor her. Devotion to her develops in us beautiful virtues, natural and Christian, such as piety, rectitude, purity, humility.

In the spiritual life of the too famous promoter of the Reformation, one omission is especially to be noticed. He holds on to Christ, our Redeemer. He even maintains that it is enough to believe in Him to be saved. God considers our faith, not our works, says Luther. *Pecca fortiter, crede fortius.* (Sin boldly and believe more boldly.) But the Blessed Virgin had no place in the mind or the heart of the apostate monk.

Hence his piety is, I do not say egotistic, but egocentric. Coiled up in himself, he thinks exclusively of his own eternal welfare. Christ is, for him, only a mediator, a means of salvation. Catholics, on the contrary, look upon Jesus with the eyes and the heart of Mary. They love Him for His benefits and also for His beauty. They contemplate Him with joy and do not tire of meditating on His perfections.

More disinterested, more loving, our piety is also more trusting. In the family, the father represents authority, the mother indulgence. When a child has committed a fault and is dreading a severe punishment, he would lose heart completely if his mother were not there to protect him. We ourselves, if we have committed mortal sins, may have been tempted to discouragement or worse. How can we expect forgiveness after having broken our word so often? Would we dare so much as lift our eyes to God? He is so great, so holy, so inexorable in exercising His justice! But in these hours of terrified bewilderment, we have remembered that we have in Heaven an Advocate, still better, a Mother; and full of hope we have implored her to intercede in our behalf.

In the Portal of the Cathedral of Rheims, Mary is depicted on her knees before the Sovereign Judge. Beside the throne of Jesus, there is an angel carrying a cross. The emblems speak for themselves. The cross, our salvation, will be also our condemnation if we do not profit by the graces it has merited for us. When we reflect that we shall have to account even for an idle word, it would be enough to terrify us if, beside our Judge, we did not see our Mother. Let us then form the habit of saying every day with a great convert: "O Mary, thou art the Mother of God, thou art also the mother of the sinner; thou art the Mother of the Judge and the mother of the culprit. Since thou art the Mother of both, let not thy guilty son be condemned by thy Son Jesus!" [1]

Mary's purity is absolute. Ours is the result of purification. Stains had to be washed away, we had to be picked up after our falls. We still have to be vigilant and use every precaution not to fall again. But the Blessed Virgin is like a crystal whose limpid clearness has never been dimmed. Erect and upright by nature, she has never needed to be straightened. In her there is no painful struggle, no wavering between good and evil. She accomplishes the Divine Will with the full consent of her whole being. She achieves perfection with sovereign ease, and with one movement reaches the heights.

Oh! how we envy her, we who are so weary of the daily fights, depressed, perhaps even disheartened at the sight of our cowardly behavior.

That is, doubtless, why men who do not believe in the

[1] St. Augustine.

Divinity of Christ, nevertheless venerate His Mother. The Mohammedans themselves visit the tomb of "The lady Mary," a monument of the Fourth Century in the Valley of Jehoshaphat, and like the Christians, they prostrate themselves before the Mother of the great prophet, Jesus.

Since we honor Mary as our Mother, devotion to her puts us and keeps us in the way of childhood, that "little Way" which, according to St. Thérèse of Lisieux, leads straight to heaven.

The child is humble; he has only to compare himself to the grown persons around him to see how small and weak he is. He is docile and confiding. It is a vital necessity for him: he would not live a month if, in his ignorance and inexperience, he tried to fend for himself.

Now these virtues of the child are also the virtues of a Christian. Imagine a man who claims to suffice for himself, to depend upon no one, to be a law unto himself; that man will have no piety, not even faith. Religion consists essentially in recognizing the authority of a superior Being from whom we have our existence, and from whom we ask light and strength. Those who claim absolute independence and rely only on themselves are impious. The chief cause of unbelief is pride. Jesus well knew this; and that is why, when He heard the Apostles disputing with each other for the first place, He said to them: "Unless ye be converted and become as little children, ye shall not enter into the Kingdom of Heaven."

Mary's influence is especially visible in those persons who have bound themselves to honor her still more than do the common of the faithful, and who by a special title are her Children. By their modesty, by their delicacy of feeling, by a certain mingling of gentleness with firmness, they may be recognized as living within the radiation of Mary's virtues. Oh! how lovely they are, these spiritual temples shining with her brightness, more beautiful than the basilicas and the cathedrals erected to her honor! After all, our churches are but heaps of stones which some day will crumble into dust, while a soul consecrated to Mary will live for ever.

In this connection, how is it possible not to admire the power of the humble Virgin of Nazareth, who even today exerts her influence over the entire world! Neither time nor distance limit her beneficent action, immense and far-reaching as her charity! . . .

Mary's faithful servants love to recite the Rosary, meditating on the Joyful, Sorrowful and Glorious Mysteries. In the truths they meditate therein, society would find the remedy for the ills it suffers.

The Mother of Jesus

The capital blunder of the modern man is that he no longer aspires to heaven. He wants his paradise in this world. Hence his horror of poverty, his dread of suffering; hence also, his inevitable and cruel disappointments. Unable to suppress accidents, sickness, infirmities, death, . . . he writhes on the cross to which he is nailed, and his contortions merely widen his wounds. Material goods have an enormous importance in his eyes. He covets them, he seeks them passionately. He envies the favorites of fortune. His dream is to dispossess them that he may enrich himself with their spoils. Cupidity arms against each other individuals, classes, nations, so that the earth, of which they would fain make an Eden, is covered with smoking ruins and drenched with blood.

How detestable this spirit of covetousness, jealousy, hatred seems to us, how wicked, how malevolent, when we piously recite the Rosary!

Mary was poor; she wore out her strength in domestic work. But this humble and laborious life was passed beneath the eyes of Jesus; and to possess Jesus is Heaven.

On Calvary, she was crucified with her Son. But she understood the worth of suffering; and far from rejecting the cross, she lovingly embraced it. Thus she merited the beautiful title of Co-Redemptrix of the human race.

After her death she was taken up to heaven, where she

enjoys the happiness so ardently desired: of rejoining her divine Son never more to be separated from Him.

Ah! how society would be transformed, how peaceful and prosperous it would become, if after Mary's example, men accepted, even loved, poverty and suffering; if they never lost sight of the purpose of life: the conquest of Heaven!

Would this esteem of the Beatitudes of the Gospel, this looking forward to our eternal future, interfere with our daily work? Not in the least. Christ Himself worked for His living, He provided bread for the hungry, a great part of His public life was spent in healing the sick. He does not forbid us to alleviate suffering, to better our condition. But He, Who is Wisdom and Harmony, puts each thing in its place. "Seek *first* the Kingdom of God and all these things shall be added unto you." Unhappily, most of us never dream of anything but *"all these things."* Of the future life they take little or no heed. They would cheerfully barter their portion of heaven for some banknotes of a thousand! Regarding as an End what should be the Means, their life is unregulated, it is a disorder, and this disorder entails suffering, it begets it. If, contrariwise, our chief concern were to please God, if His Holy Law were observed by all, it would be the end of discords, quarrels, wars. Justice and Charity would lead back to us once more their gentle companion, Peace. This is the teaching of the Rosary: let us hope that our century may at last understand it and put it in practice.

In the Middle Ages pilgrims going by sea to the Holy Land used to invoke Mary morning and evening. At dawn, the Captain would set up on the poop an image of the Madonna, and the pilgrims on their knees recited thrice the Ave Maria. At nightfall, they again assembled around the holy image and devoutly sang the Salve Regina. They were exposed to great dangers on the voyage, but they hoped to reach port in safety, because Mary was watching over them.

We, too, are pilgrims, crossing the sea of life, hoping to weather its storms and safely make port in Heaven. Who should be our Guide, our Pilot, if not Mary? Like our pious ancestors, let us invoke her morning and evening. Let us implore her to succor us in our troubles, in our temptations, and especially in our last agony. Death will be less bitter for us if we are helped by our heavenly Mother. May we die murmuring the first word man learns to say and the last on his lips, "Mother!"

XXVIII

Our Heavenly Mother

God is love, and wishing to make man to His own image and likeness, He put into his heart . . . Goodness, or "loving-kindness," as it was called in England in medieval days.

What is true of man in general is truer of Mary, the most perfect likeness of God ever seen in this world, had the Word not become Incarnate.

When God made the body and soul of Mary, He adorned them with the qualities which later were to shine forth so brilliantly in Jesus. Now which is the first virtue of Christ, the one He first recommends and most emphasizes, if not charity?

Let us remember that Mary was both Teacher and Disciple of her divine Son. During the hidden life, Jesus performed no unusual action, He did not speak in public. But if He did not teach the multitudes, He instructed His own family. If He is not yet a star in the firmament, He is a lamp in the home. How can we imagine that He did not permit some beams to filter through from that focus of light that was in Him? When they found Him again in the Temple, Mary was struck by the words that He said; but she must have kept many another that the Gospels have not recorded.

We love to picture to ourselves the Holy Family praying together. After a hard day's work, the thoughts of Jesus turn to the future. He thinks of the Kingdom of God that He is going to found; and to whom would He confide His hopes if not to His Mother? He opens out new horizons to her; He gives her a glimpse of a more perfect Law than the Mosaic. "You have heard it said: Thou shalt not kill. But I say unto you, whosoever is angry with his brother, shall be in danger of the judgment. And whosoever shall say, Thou fool, shall be in danger of hell-fire. You have heard that it hath been said, Thou shalt love thy neighbor and hate thy enemy. But I say to you, Love your enemies; do good to them that hate you and pray for them that persecute you. Do unto others as you would have them do unto you."

That Mary was penetrated by these teachings is clearly shown in the Gospel. At the wedding-feast of Cana, she notices the predicament of the young couple. She intervenes in their behalf with delicate grace, and her charity calls forth the first miracle recorded in the Gospel.

Suffering patiently borne makes the soul compassionate.

Why are so many children hard and unsympathetic with their comrades and those at home? Young boys are ruthless, because they know nothing as yet of the pains and hardships of life. But the Blessed Virgin was cruelly tried. We rightly call her the Queen of Martyrs. The higher the degree of perfection to which God calls a soul, the more important the mission He confides to her, the more tribulations He sends her. This Law, which stands out in the lives of saints with terrible evidence, was expressed by one who returned from the World War in a striking way: "The size of our cross is the measure of our greatness." [1]

If this be true, how intensely Our Lady must have suffered, she, the most perfect of women; she, the Saviour's Mother, the Co-Redemptrix of the world! The weight of her cross was in proportion to her exalted dignity.

But precisely because she suffered so poignantly, she knows how to compassionate our woes. She understands us at once as soon as we pour out our hearts to her as our Mother. Like one of Virgil's heroes she might say: "Having known misfortune myself, I know how to pity the unfortunate." *Non ignara malis, miseris succurrere disco.*

This idea has been admirably symbolized by one of those unknown artists who, before the Revolution, en-

[1] Jacques d'Arnoux.

riched our churches with so many masterpieces. Upon a promontory of the Morbihan, close to the sea, rises a sanctuary dedicated to Our Lady. It is not a chapel, not even an oratory, but a simple niche protected from the winds by some stunted shrubs. The niche shelters an ancient statue in wood representing Our Lady of Seven Dolors. Her heart is transpierced by the swords. Beside her the divine Child, leaning on an anchor, the emblem of hope, points upward to Heaven. This group is eloquent. To the sailors' wives who come to seek from her a little consolation, Mary stretches out her arms as if saying: "Come without fear! Look at my wounded heart. I know what it means to suffer. Pray to my divine Son; He will console you." And by His gesture, by His whole attitude, Jesus says: "Hope! there above is Heaven!"

If we now wish to know how the "loving-kindness" of the Blessed Virgin shows itself, let us revert to her Litanies.

We invoke her under the title Health of the Sick. Poor infirm persons, the sick poor, lying in their solitary rooms or in the common wards of hospitals, if they are believers, can be seen passing their beads through their fingers during many a long, sleepless hour. Mary hastens to them as a mother to the bedside of her sick child; and while they feel the sweetness of her presence, their brow is less burning with fever, their heart less heavy with sadness.

When Jesus was passing through the hamlets of Palestine, He healed all sickness and infirmity. Have we not a similar spectacle under our very eyes? From every corner of France, and even of Europe, the sick and infirm throng to Massabielle. They are carried or wheeled to the basilica, in front of the grotto where the Immaculate appeared. And it is not in vain that they entreat her, for the heavenly wonder-worker sends them home either cured or comforted.

Here again, you are, O Mary, the Consoler of the Afflicted.

A modern painter has represented you in a mourning garb, seated on a throne.

A young woman with disheveled hair and disordered garments has cast herself upon you and is hiding her face in your bosom, poor unfortunate creature! lest she see a fearful sight, her child lying dead on the ground. And you, with eyes and hands raised to heaven, are drawing down upon this desolate mother the sweetness of your consolations.

Thus when a disaster strikes us down, when grief overwhelms us, when fear paralyzes us, we cast it all at your feet. We cry out to you, poor banished children of Eve, exiled in this valley of tears, and we shall not cease to call you to our aid until you turn your eyes of mercy towards us, O clement, O loving, O sweet Virgin, Mary!

Of all the afflicted, those who hold the first place in our minds and hearts are, perhaps, the deceased who are still expiating their sins. You do not abandon any of your children, but your compassion leans particularly towards those of the Church Suffering. Doubtless you can not relieve them of all pain; suffering is beneficent when endured for love of God. It is necessary to purify souls, to embellish them, to clothe them in that "nuptial garment" without which they can not be admitted to the heavenly banquet. But by your prayers you sustain their courage, you revive their hope. Captivity becomes less painful to them in the thought that a Mother is interested in them and will soon welcome them on the threshold of paradise. O merciful Virgin, continue to assist our dear departed, offer for them our merits and our prayers.

Languentibus in Purgatorio,
Qui purgantur ardore nimio
Et torquentur gravi supplicio,
Subveniat tua compassio,
O Maria! [1]

[1] Let thy compassion come to the help of those languishing in Purgatory, who are being cleansed in fiery flames and writhe in bitter torment, O Mary!

The Litanies call you also the Refuge of Sinners. Is it not a wonderful thing that you should attract at once the purest souls and the most defiled? This hardened sinner who dares not lift his eyes to the Heavenly Father, has not lost confidence in you. He who never sets foot in a church, wears your medal and kisses it every night. He is touched by the memory of that beautiful day when he consecrated himself for life to the Queen of Heaven. It is you on whom he relies to obtain his forgiveness, to help him to rise again. Nor is his hope groundless. How many souls whose plight seemed desperate have you not rescued from the mire! How many prodigals have you not brought back to the Father's house! One of them thus expressed his gratitude to you:

> Henceforth my Mother, Mary, my only love shall be,
> For in my foolish wickedness and guilty weakness, she
> Taught my bold eyes to drop, my hands to fold,
> My lips to sigh th' adoring words she told! [1]

To sum up, Mary is our Mother. What sweetness the word contains! A mother is watchful tenderness, unbounded indulgence, undaunted devotedness. As long as a child feels his mother's protection, life seems good to him. He does not worry about the future, for it is being taken care of for him. We can thus say with the old poet:

[1] Paul Verlaine.

221

> Each one must fondly yearn
>> To turn
> To thee, O Gracious, Fair!
> All good to love, all evil spurn,
>> Will learn,
> Who seeks thine aid in Prayer!

Yet, let us often call upon Mary, as a child calls his mother when he is hurt, when he is frightened. We may be quite sure that she will not be deaf to our entreaties. If she can not give us perfect happiness, which is not possible in this life, she will obtain peace for us that peace of God which is like a foretaste of eternal rest.

XXIX

MARY, QUEEN OF FRANCE

CHRIST reigns by right over all men, because He is our Creator, our Redeemer. He actually reigns over all those who recognize His Divinity, that is to say, over six hundred millions of human beings. Mary, His Mother, is the Queen of this immense empire. All Christians are her children. Our forefathers, however, were not mistaken in calling her "Queen of France," since she is nowhere better served than in our country even in our own day, and always has been. Besides one of our Kings consecrated himself and his Kingdom to her.

As far back as the age of the Druids, long before the seeds of the Gospel had been sown in Gaul, our ancestors venerated in a grotto in the depths of the forest the statue of a woman holding a child in her lap. This statue, which afterwards, under the name of Our Lady of Chartres, was to have so many faithful devotees, to see prostrate before her so many great lords and even Kings, bore on its pedestal the mysterious inscription: "To the Virgin who is to give birth."

Thus, it would appear that before Our Lord was born, the Druids had a presentiment of the glory of her who was to bring Him into the world. Was it a tradition transmitted from the beginnings of Humanity? Was it an echo of Jewish beliefs and of the prophecy of Isaias: "Behold a Virgin shall conceive and shall bring forth a Son, and his name shall be called Emmanuel"? We do not know; but it is a noteworthy fact that this presentiment of the Virginity of the Mother of God and of the honor thenceforth paid to the Virgin should be found so early in this country where she was later to reign.

This obscure seed dropped by God into French soil, was to sprout in the Middle Ages, push its way up and come to magnificent flowering. In that remote period, when passions were so violent, manners so rough and uncouth, a sentiment was growing,—like a flower in the cleft of a rock,—a sentiment pure and tender: love for Mary. By thousands, serfs and lords, statesmen and warriors, began to shut themselves up in cloisters. Far from the tumult of the world and the bustle of business, they contemplated in prayer and labor her whose beauty had captivated them and whom they had chosen as the "Lady of their thoughts."

Artists dreamed of her; and with chisel or palette in hand tried to preserve in stone or on canvas the divine image that hovered before their inward eye like a heavenly vision.

And what shall we say of the thousands of shrines built to the honor of the Virgin in the Eleventh Century and in succeeding ages! Who can count the splendid monuments, masterpieces of our national architecture, Our Lady of Rouen, Our Lady of Rheims, Our Lady of Amiens, Our Lady of Paris: colossal structures, the works of a whole people, poems in stone, whose carved portals and flamboyant windows so eloquently attest our forefathers' veneration of the Virgin Mary.

How touching also are the Mystery Plays of the Middle Ages, especially the Miracle Plays of Our Lady! These were dramas usually acted in the open square before the Church, at the expense of the town and with the co-operation of pious Guilds or Brotherhoods. Now of all the dramas of this sort composed in the Fourteenth Century, which have come down to us, there is not one that is not in honor of the Virgin. The subject is uniformly the same. A notorious criminal, having drunk deep of shame, and wallowed in every mire, has fallen into the hands of human justice. Seeing himself face to face with horrible death and the flames of Hell beyond, he feels the necessity of repentance, and murmurs with trembling lips an Ave Maria. Mary hastens to his aid, bends over the wretch, dries his tears and transforms him into a holy penitent.

It was not artists and poets only who honored the Virgin in those days. Theologians paid her another sort of homage: they erected spiritual temples to her glory, which implies, not greater love, assuredly, but wider knowledge. From the works of St. Hilary, St. Anselm, St. Bernard, how many beautiful pages we might cite, which would be like a sheaf of flowers offered to her! It is also a remarkable fact that already in the Thirteenth Century the University of Paris declared its belief in the Immaculate Conception. It ardently defended this thesis, which was not yet an article of faith. We still recite a prayer attributed to one of its Doctors. When he was about to plead the cause of his Immaculate Queen, he raised his eyes to her image, murmuring: *Dignare me laudare te, Virgo sacrata; da mihi virtutem contra hostes tuos.* "Make me worthy to praise thee, O holy Virgin! Give me strength against thy adversaries!"

The story of Jeanne d'Arc shows clearly how popular was the devotion to the Blessed Virgin in the Middle Ages. As a child she loved to recite the Angelus; she even gave wool from her sheep to the sacristan, to induce him to be more punctual in ringing the evening Angelus. She often visited the shrine of Our Lady of the Oak; and not being able to go to Our Lady of Puy for the Jubilee, she begged her mother to make the pilgrimage in her stead. She called herself the messenger of Mary. "I come," she said, "in the Name of God, of the Virgin, and of all the blessed Saints of paradise." We know her beautiful motto: "Jhesus, Maria." She wrote or dictated these two names at the head of all her letters. They were engraved on a ring that she wore on her finger and piously kissed when in danger. She had them embroidered on her triangular pennon, on which was represented the Mystery of the Annunciation.

Thus, long before the vow of Louis XIII, Mary was reigning as Sovereign in the land of France, and although her Queenship had not yet been proclaimed, it existed in fact. By its monuments, by its literature, by its frequent pilgrimages, France manifested for centuries its intention to consecrate itself to the Queen of Heaven.

Louis XIII deserves credit for having understood this popular movement and given it official sanction. On February 10, 1638, he issued Letters Patent, in which after having recalled the titles and favors of Mary, he concludes in these terms:

"For these causes, we have declared and do declare that, taking the Most Holy and glorious Virgin as special Patroness of our Kingdom, we consecrate to her particularly our person, our State, our Crown, and our Subjects." It would be difficult to exaggerate the importance of such a document.

Let us remark first that it was, if not written, at least signed by an absolute monarch, whose decisions had the force of law. Representing the French nation, Louis XIII spoke in its name. According to the ideas of the time, France was his domain: he had, therefore, the right to offer it to Mary.

The better to grasp the significance of this act, it is well to recall the distinction so familiar in the Middle Ages between vassal and suzerain. The vassal was a landed proprietor; but he held his land (fief) from another lord more powerful than he, to whom he had to do homage and render service. When, on the insistence of Jeanne d'Arc, Charles VII offered his Kingdom to Christ Jesus, he recognized Him as suzerain, and declared himself ready to defend His cause. Likewise, when in a chapel of Abbéville, Louis XIII offered Mary his scepter and his crown, he proclaimed her Queen of France.[1] The cele-

[1] TRANSLATOR'S NOTE: France is not alone in that mark of honor to Our Lady. Bavaria claims her as Queen and the national flag is light-blue and

brated Grotius, then Swedish Ambassador to France, understood this very well. In a letter inspired by his Lutheran prejudice, he contended that in consecrating his Kingdom to the Virgin Mary, the King, Louis XIII, had violated the Salic Law, which excludes women from the French throne!

Lastly, note that here there is no question of a private act, like vows we formulate in the secrecy of our own conscience. The Letters Patent of February 10, 1638, were registered by the Parliament, and to associate the entire nation in his pious initiative, Louis XIII ordained that this great act should be commemorated on the Feast of the Assumption by a solemn procession.

He was enthusiastically obeyed: the people walked in their sovereign's footsteps. In all the monasteries, in every parochial church of the kingdom, this Feast of August 15, 1638, was celebrated with unwonted splendor. Nor was this a mere flaring-up of enthusiasm; our devotion to Mary is as constant as it is fervent.

The oldest among us may perhaps remember the gorgeousness which used formerly to characterize the Mid-August Feast. In the great cities especially, the Virgin Mary received extraordinary marks of honor. Civic Au-

white, Our Lady's colors. Hungary also claims her by the same title. Both countries add "Regina Bavariae" and "Regina Ungariae" as the last invocation to the Litany of Loretto. See Translator's Note, p. vii.

thorities, State Officials, the Corporations escorted her, and the Procession advanced between two files of soldiers, the chanting of the priests alternating with the military bands.

It is no longer so in our day. The State pays no official homage to Mary. If Magistrates assist at religious services, it is in their private capacity as individuals, not as representatives of the nation or any part of it. In spite of everything, however, the Feast of Mid-August still retains its popularity. The very mention of it evokes the great souvenirs of our history and strikes a vibrant chord in French hearts. If in the eyes of the powers that be, it is no longer a National Feast, in our minds and in our hearts it will always be the Feast of France.

It is consoling to think that the first act of the Pontificate of Pius XI was a Bull, published in March, 1922, in which Mary is recognized as the chief Patroness of France. Thus the vow of Louis XIII has been confirmed by the Supreme Authority of the Church.

Such memories should revive our confidence, should they not? Many of the faithful recalling their consecration to Mary on their First Communion Day, say to her fervently: "Since therefore I am thine, O sweetest Mother, watch over me and protect me as thy property and possession."

For centuries then France has been Mary's property, her land. Let us hope that our Sovereign will defend it against its enemies and bring back to us peace and prosperity.

XXX

What France Owes to Mary

One day the Immaculate Virgin told Bernadette to dig in the sand near the grotto. The child obeyed and beheld a copious spring gush forth. Is not this water which since then has never ceased to flow and has cured so many sick and infirm, an image of the countless graces that Mary showers over the whole world and particularly upon France? Devotion to her has had a happy influence upon our country. Her powerful intercession has saved us many a time. The recollection of so many favors is a consolation for us and encourages us to hope.

During the Middle Ages an institution was founded which played an important part in our history. At that time warfare was well-nigh continual; city fought against city; castle against castle. The King was powerless to control the "Great Companies" of bandits and scoundrels who infested all the roads, lying in wait for travelers and holding them for ransom. In this general triumph of brute force what became of the rights of the weak? The widow, the orphan, the old, . . . to whom could they appeal for defense? Were they to be left exposed helpless to the ruthless cruelty of brigands?"

It was then that Chivalry sprang up; an association of noble warriors who bound themselves not to draw the sword save in defense of the oppressed and to safeguard the weak. A great institution it was, upon which some writers have heaped ridicule, but which in its day rendered incalculable services to civilization.

Now in reading the chronicles of that epoch one thing strikes even the least attentive; it is the devotion of the Knights to the Virgin Mary. It was to give honor to Mary that they donned the cuirass and drew the sword. For love of her they fared forth to distant lands, braving all perils and dying with joy. If a Knight seemed about to hesitate or weaken: "In the Virgin's name!" they said to him, "be not recreant to your oath!" At that reminder the Knight would brace himself and repent; he would ask pardon of God for having listened to the suggestion of the evil spirit, and thank his Lady Mary who had saved him from dishonor.

Can we be surprised at the abnegation, the generosity of these valiant men? In their practice of virtue, they were but imitating their Queen. Mary so loved mankind that for its salvation she gave her only Son. Noble examples

233

are proverbially contagious. If it is true that a soul that loves, communicates something of its generosity to those around it, one can understand what influence Mary exerts over her devoted servitors, and how in imitating her they become self-forgetful, full of charity for others, in a word, chivalrously devoted.

This beneficent influence of Mary was not concentrated in a single association, nor limited to a single period of our history; it is the whole of France that has benefited by it. One of its distinctive characteristics is pity for all suffering, generous indignation against the excesses of triumphant force. If two nations are at war, it is not to the stronger, to the one most sure of victory, that her sympathy goes out; but to the one that is defending its rights, that is fighting for its honor and liberty. And when it is force that has conquered, when the weaker lies prostrate, disarmed and helpless, France bends over it compassionately to alleviate the bitterness of defeat.

Where did we get that delicacy, that generosity, which so long have been the glory of France in the eyes of the civilized world? Did we not find it at Mary's feet? Our forefathers venerated her so deeply! So many generations have prayed before her image! She has opened so many hearts to pity and love, that a fund of generosity has remained in the French soul that will never disappear.

234

We were speaking just now of the Middle Ages. There is another epoch in our history not less troublous; it is the epoch of the Wars of Religion. Once it had gained a foothold, Protestantism made rapid progress. Armed bands roamed through the country to support the cause of heresy. Daily quarrels between Catholics and Huguenots embittered both sides. Soon what began as local disorders developed into Civil War, and the conflagration spread all over France.

But the Virgin was watching over her kingdom. She could not permit it to fall into the hands of a heretical sect. It is she who preserved our faith.

Here is a significant fact relative to this subject. Some years ago a Protestant minister came to give a public controversial lecture in a commune of the Côtes du Nord. Perturbed by the danger to the faith of his parishioners, since he had been forbidden to engage in a public debate with the minister, the Catholic priest merely announced at High Mass: "My brethren, strangers have come here to preach a new religion. I have but one word to say to you; these persons have no love for the Blessed Virgin."

The warning was effective; the minister had not a single Catholic at his lecture.

"These persons have no love for the Blessed Virgin." Do not these words of the Breton Curé throw a clear light on the religious history of our country? Protestants pay no public honor to Mary; that is the main reason why they have never triumphed in our land. The French might have been able to accept other errors; in questions of religion it is so easy to make a mistake. But when they saw the Huguenots burning the statues and pictures of the Blessed Virgin and overturning her altars, they instinctively distrusted them. To be a Frenchman and not love Mary was impossible; and France remained Catholic in order not to deny her Queen.

If now we cast a glance over the general course of our history, we shall perceive that in more than one critical situation Mary intervened in our behalf.

In the year 885, the Normans laid siege to Paris, thinking it unable to defend itself. A man of tremendous energy, the Bishop Goslin, organized the resistance, and at the end of eleven months the enemy grew discouraged and abandoned the siege. The Parisians attributed their deliverance, not to the reinforcements they had received, but to Mary's intervention. In a hymn that has come down to us, we read: "O Normans, it is not the Frank that defeated you, not the Burgundian that cut you to pieces; it is the Virgin Mary, our Queen."

In 1214, the Flemings and the Germans invaded France,

236

Philip Augustus gave battle to them at Bouvines. He was victorious; and to show his gratitude he laid the first stone of the Cathedral of Our Lady of Paris.

In 1360, the English besieged Chartres, Mary's city. But a frightful storm burst upon them and decimated them. Their King, Edward III, vowed to make peace if God would spare the rest of his army. He kept his word, and shortly after signed the Peace of Brétigny.

Before beginning his campaign, the first Chief of the League, Jacques d'Humières, went in pilgrimage to Our Lady of Brébières, and besought the Blessed Virgin's assistance in his enterprise. His prayer was granted. After ups and downs, successes and reverses, the League finally accomplished its purpose, since it prevented the Huguenots from seizing control of the Government.

Before besieging La Rochelle, where the Protestants had entrenched themselves, Louis XIII promised Our Lady, if she blessed his arms, to build her a church in his capital; it is the ever venerated Our Lady of Victories.

Here is another memorable fact that happened during the Crimean War. The siege of Sebastopol was dragging on interminably. To put an end to it, the Malakoff Tower, a very strong position, had to be stormed. Pélissier decided to make the assault on September 8th, Mary's Birthday. In vain the strong-minded indignantly protested against what they sneered at as his bigotry. The Malakoff Tower was taken, and the Capitulation followed.[1]

In our own days, Mary has given us still more famous signs of her maternal benevolence. We allude to the three apparitions of La Salette, Lourdes and Pontmain. There is a manifest connection between these three messages; they introduce and complete each other. Behold her on the mountain of La Salette. She is seated, her bowed head in her hands, she is weeping. "I can not restrain my Son's arm," she says to the shepherds listening to her, "Men blaspheme His Name. On Sunday instead of hearing Mass, they go to their fields or to their workshops. That is why my Son's arm is so heavy."

And at Lourdes, continuing in the same strain, she points out how the threatening disaster may be averted. She repeats three times, with increasing emphasis, that word so dreaded by Christians in our day: "Penance! Penance! Penance!!"

Alas! France (official France at least) remained deaf to Mary's warning. France went her own way, without seeing on the horizon the black cloud to which Mary was pointing.

The chastisement was not slow in coming and it was

[1] See in the *Idéal*, November, 1911, *Les Victoires de Notre Dame,* by S. Coubé.

terrible. The War of 1870 was but a series of defeats and capitulations. At the end of this heavy trial, Mary appeared again to console us and to exhort us to repentance and prayer. "God will soon hear your prayers," she said to the children of Pontmain. In fact, eleven days later, the armistice was signed.

Let us recall what happened at the outset of the World War. In August, 1914, France was again invaded. After some days of a triumphal march, the Germans were but twenty leagues from Paris. If von Klück had wished, he could have entered the capital without striking a blow. But he thought it wiser to encircle our defeated army and end the war by a master-stroke. It was then that occurred that prodigious straightening and stiffening of the French army which is called "the miracle of the Marne." And it was precisely on September 8th, Mary's Birthday, that our victorious defensive was unleashed!

"Pure coincidence!" say the free-thinkers, shrugging their shoulders. "The victory of the Marne is explained by a multitude of happy chances." Let them content themselves with this childish and improbable explanation, it is their own affair. We, who know that there is no such thing as chance, can see in this event which decided our fate, a providential intervention. Once again, Mary saved us.

The Mother of Jesus

From all these facts there stands out a comforting reassurance. Like the ship that is the symbol of the City of Paris, France is often tempest-tossed, but she does not sink! *Fluctuat nec mergitur!*

You remember those fine words spoken by Charlemagne in *La Fille de Roland:* "France, we must never despair of thee!" No, we must never despair of France, for after the worst reverses, after the Norman invasions, after the Hundred Years' War, after the horrors of the Revolution, after the disaster of Charleroi, she has always risen again, bruised but confident. France has more resources than her enemies dream, more even than her own children know. It must never be said of her: "It is finished, her last hour has struck," for what the prophets of misfortune take for the passing-bell, may well turn out to be triumphal chimes announcing the resurrection.

Our confidence is not based on historical reasons only; it is grounded more solidly on our faith. We believe that the Queen of France will not abandon this fair domain entrusted to her by Louis XIII. We believe that if she has saved us so many times, it was not to let us perish in the end.

Let us then follow the counsel she gave to the children of Pontmain; let us pray with all our heart, and work our hardest, and God will save us by His own means, providential means, worth more than our short-sighted wisdom could even imagine!

Of course, we can not help feeling sad and depressed at times; we have such urgent need of peace and security! But if we are tempted to discouragement, let us remind ourselves of the bold word of a great Pope, Benedict XIV, *Regnum Mariae nunquam peribit.* "Mary's Kingdom shall never perish!"

XXXI

APPARITIONS OF THE BLESSED VIRGIN

IN THE space of a quarter of a century, from 1846 to 1871, Mary created in our country three new centers of pilgrimage: La Salette, Lourdes, Pontmain. Not being able to favor every village and every hamlet in her vast domain, the Blessed Virgin selected three points rather far apart forming a glorious triangle on French soil.

We shall not speak of the messages she brought us. What interests us to-day is the manner of the apparitions. As a thing acts, so it is. The way in which the Blessed Virgin manifested herself reveals her character therefore, and will complete or at least confirm what we have learned from the Gospel.

The first thing that strikes us in the apparitions is a wholly heavenly beauty. At Lourdes, a mysterious light announced each visit of the Immaculate, like the aurora that precedes the rising of a star. At Pontmain, Mary was surrounded by a white aureola in oval shape. Stars shone around her and beneath her feet, a shining background that befits the Queen of Heaven.

Her voice is clear and sweet, her gestures graceful. She has a charming way of greeting and of making the sign of the Cross. Instinctively Bernadette imitates her. For five months she goes to Mary's school, and learns from her good manners.

"The Virgin is beautiful," she said one day. "When one has once seen her, one longs to die." Everything seems dull and drab in comparison with her ideal loveliness, and the world would be unendurable if we had not the hope of seeing her again. In the Convent at Nevers, Bernadette was asked whether the statue placed in the grotto looked anything like her. "Yes," she replied, not without irony, "it is like her, about as like as earth is like Heaven."

The apparition of Pontmain gives the same impression of supernatural beauty. "How beautiful it is! How beautiful!" the children kept repeating. One of them said later, and his naïve expression is strangely energetic: "One would have liked to jump up to her!" The adults present, unable to endure the icy cold, sought refuge in a barn. The children who saw her did not feel the biting wind. For three hours that passed like a flash of lightning for them, they kept their eyes fixed on "the beautiful lady." In ecstasy, beside themselves, they were transported into another world. A heavenly gate had opened, revealing one of the visions that ravish the Blessed.

The Virgin does not appear, however, in the imposing majesty of a sovereign. Charming in her simplicity, she attracts rather than intimidates. She smiles when Bernadette throws some holy water on her to assure herself that the vision is not a ruse of the devil. And when the little shepherdess offers her a sheet of paper and a pen to write her name, Mary smiles again at her artless ingenuousness. Full of consideration for the poor little girl, she speaks to her with kind courtesy, "Will you have the goodness to come here daily for fifteen days?" Bernadette can not get over her astonishment at being addressed with so much respect. Mary takes no notice of her social rank, of her shabby clothes, of her rustic speech, but considers only her supernatural dignity. Is not every soul in the state of grace a sanctuary in which the Blessed Trinity resides?

At Pontmain as at Lourdes, Mary showed herself benevolent and motherly. She opened her hands and lowered them towards the earth, as though showering graces. She smiled while the consoling inscription was forming at her feet: "God will soon hear your prayers." This smile was so sweet, that involuntarily the children imitated it. A heavenly reflection lighted up their faces.

What is most astonishing, perhaps, in these apparitions is their perfect propriety. Everything about them is foreseen and ordained by a superhuman wisdom.

In his celebrated Pietà, Michelangelo gives his Madonna a youthfulness that surprises us at first. At the time of the Passion she was about fifty years old. But according to the remark of the great artist himself, the Immaculate Virgin, untouched by any shadow of sin, has ever the freshness of a newly opened flower. Since her Assumption, Mary has been living in a land that knows no evening. We call "old" those who are approaching the end of their earthly existence, but for the immortals there is no end, therefore no decline. They are always young, for their lives are always at the dawn. Now we understand why the Blessed Virgin when she vouchsafes to visit us, appears so young; sixteen, says Bernadette, from eighteen to twenty say the children of Pontmain.

When Bernadette recited the Hail Mary, the Virgin did not move her lips; it is not fitting that she should honor herself, but she pronounced the words of the Gloria Patri, for she, like the Pyrenean shepherdess, must pay homage to the Blessed Trinity.

During her prayer, Mary did not raise her eyes to heaven. This gesture is a survival of ancient times when the sojourn of the Blessed was supposed to be in the empyrean. To-day we know that there is no up nor down, no high nor low in space. What is above our heads at noon is under our feet at midnight; Heaven is not the zenith; it is the possession of God. Why seek *above,* Him Who is everywhere?

At Lourdes, the Virgin appeared during the day, at Pontmain, during the night; in the former apparition she wore a white robe with a blue girdle; in the latter, a dark blue robe and a black veil. The reason of these differences is sufficiently evident.

Why did the Virgin appear at Lourdes? For several reasons doubtless, but especially to confirm the doctrine defined four years previously. "I am the Immaculate Conception," she said to Bernadette. Thus in the apparition of Lourdes everything bespeaks innocence, purity: the Virgin's garments, the golden roses opening at her feet, the miraculous spring gushing forth near the grotto.

At Pontmain, the Virgin announces the end of a great trial. In a few days the armistice will be signed. But as yet France is in agony. Paris, starving, is discussing surrender. The German troops are marching on Laval. In her delicate sympathy, Mary associates herself with the mourning of the nation whose sovereign she is. The stars twinkling around her, the shining gold letters of the inscription bring out by contrast the somber robe and veil. The red thread that adorns her diadem, the Crucifix she shows the children, recall to our minds a solemn and terrible law in the supernatural order: it is that without the shedding of blood there is no remission.

At Lourdes, Mary presents herself as the Immaculate Conception; that is why she wears no crown. At Pontmain, she speaks as Mother of God. "My Son lets Himself be touched . . ." she says. Now the Mother of a King shares his dignity, and to adopt some of his insignia is permissible to her.

The same propriety is manifest in the choice of witnesses. They are quite young, . . . children. They are surrounded by adults who envy without sharing their happy privilege. At Pontmain, the Curé of the Parish, a holy man, and the Sisters teaching in the school, are surprised and a bit humiliated at seeing nothing. The Immaculate reveals herself to those only who resemble her, to children whose innocence has preserved them from all sin and even from temptation.

These children are the offspring of workmen or peasants. They lead a humble, laborious life. The Virgin of Nazareth, like her Divine Son, has a marked preference for the poor.

These children are very simple. They speak the patois (dialect) of their section of the country. Their instruction is most summary. God so willed, in order to render their testimony indubitable. How could anyone believe that little peasants of Pontmain could stage a drama in which every detail is pregnant with significance? How believe that they could have devised the inscription in capital letters conformably with epigraphy but not with the rules taught them at school?

These children love God with all their heart. Bernadette becomes indignant when she hears blasphemy. Every day the little Barbedettes recite the rosary for their brother at the Front. Every morning very early they go to Church and make the Way of the Cross, before serving Mass.

They are good, pious children, not mystics. The apparition of July 16, 1858, was the last for Bernadette, and for the children of Pontmain, that of January 17, 1871, was the only one. They were not, therefore, temperamental visionaries. Nothing had prepared them for an exceptional favor which it did not please Providence to repeat.

At Lourdes the Virgin spoke, while at Pontmain she wrote. That is because at the latter place there were six children who saw her. They might have misunderstood her words, misconstrued them, or contradicted each other, and such contradictions would have greatly decreased the value of their testimony if not completely invalidated it. Foreseeing these difficulties, the Virgin Most Prudent

248

forestalled them, . . . she wrote her message. She wrote it very slowly, letter by letter, so that these children, accustomed to spelling, might decipher it without trouble.

Finally, let us notice that, following the rules of sound pedagogy, Mary *shows* the truth she teaches, rather than *states* it. She puts before the children's eyes symbolic pictures, leaving it to them, or to better educated persons, to interpret them.

Those who had the privilege of seeing and venerating the Blessed Virgin in the days of her earthly pilgrimage, would have recognized her perfectly at La Salette, at Lourdes, and at Pontmain. She has not changed her character. Beauty that charms the senses in order to lift up the soul, maternal benevolence, courtesy, delicate refinement, deep wisdom, are the characteristics we admire in the Gospel and in the Virgin of the Apparitions. Is not this remarkable concordance a proof of authenticity? Error is fated to give itself the lie, but truth is always consistent with itself.

Thus the Virgin really did appear in the land of France. Her feet have touched our soil. Happy witnesses have gazed upon her face, have listened to her voice. May we appreciate this favor and make ourselves worthy of it!

The Mother of Jesus

Oh! may the day dawn when France, abjuring the errors that have exercised so sinister an influence upon her, may again become what she was in the glorious days of Saint Louis; the Knight of God, the Defender of His Rights, the faithful Servant of Jesus and of His Mother!